Modern Floriography

Flowers, Gardens, & Gifts
Inspired by the Language
of Flowers

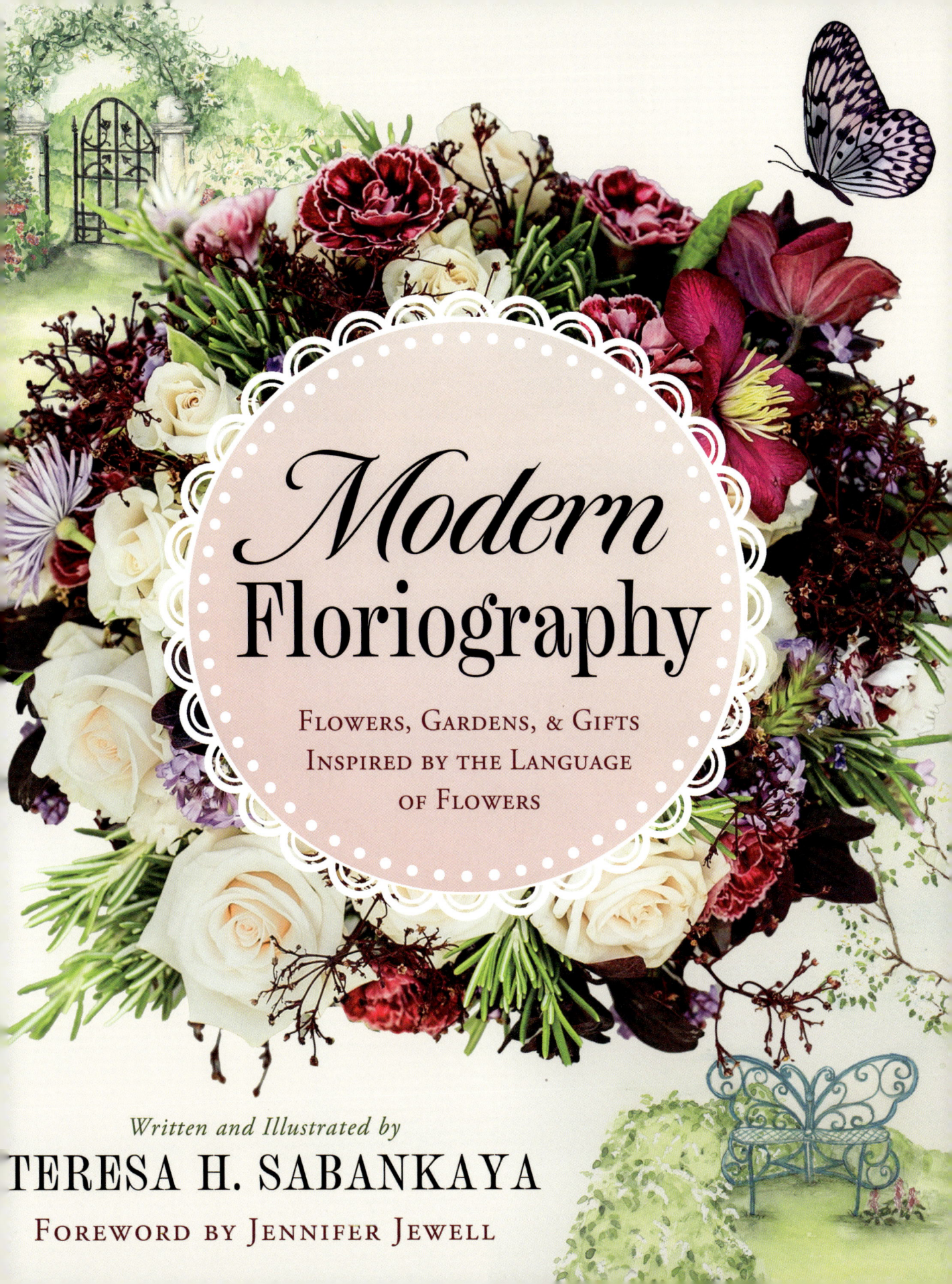

Modern Floriography: Flowers, Gardens, and Gifts Inspired by the Language of Flowers

© 2026 by Teresa H. Sabankaya

All rights reserved. No portion of this publication may be reproduced, stored in a retrieval system, or transmitted by any means—electronic, mechanical, photocopying, recording, or any other—except for brief quotations in printed reviews, without the prior written permission of the publisher.

Library of Congress Control Number: 2025912725

ISBN: 978-1-964686-67-7 (hardcover) 978-1-964686-68-4 (ebook)

Although this publication is designed to provide accurate information about the subject matter, the publisher and the author assume no responsibility for any errors, inaccuracies, omissions, or inconsistencies herein. This publication is intended as a resource, however, it is not intended as a replacement for direct and personalized professional services.

Editors: Marci Carson, Juliann Barbato
Photography: Anne Renée LaPlante
Illustrations: Teresa Sabankaya
Cover and Interior Design: Emma Elzinga
Printed in the United States of America

Quote from The Well Gardened Mind by Sue Stuart Smith, page 63
Reprinted by permission of HarperCollins Publishers Ltd
© 2020 by Sue Stuart Smith

First Edition

Indigo River Publishing
3 West Garden Street, Ste. 718
Pensacola, FL 32502
www.indigoriverpublishing.com

Ordering Information:

Quantity sales: Special discounts are available on quantity purchases by corporations, associations, and others. For details, contact the publisher at the address above.

Orders by US trade bookstores and wholesalers: Please contact the publisher at the address above.

With Indigo River Publishing, you can always expect great books, strong voices, and meaningful messages. Most importantly, you'll always find . . . *words worth reading.*

Besides my beloved family and faithful friends, there has been no greater love in my life than flowers and gardens. And specifically, their ability to impart eloquent tidings to us, and to heal and nurture us in so many ways.

I dedicate this book to all of you who will find the time to be quiet and pay attention to the plants, trees, and flowers, and the brilliant language they speak to us. May they continue to prompt us all to savor nature and its abundant gifts to us.

—Teresa

Table of Contents

FOREWORD	XIII
INTRODUCTION: A TIMELY REVIVAL	XV
HOW TO USE THIS BOOK	XVI
GETTING ACQUAINTED WITH FLORIOGRAPHY	XIX
Ancient Egypt	XX
Ancient Greece and Rome	XXI
Medieval Times	XXIII
Renaissance Period	XXV
Victorian Era	XXVI
LITERATURE, PLAYWRIGHTS, AND PRE-RAPHAELITE ARTWORKS	XXVI
Modern History	XXVII
PART 1: DAY-TO-DAY FLORIOGRAPHY	1
EN MASSE BOUQUETS	3
Baby's Breath	4
Calla Lily	5
Cosmos	7
Daffodil	8
Dahlia	9
Hellebore	10

Lady's Mantle	11
Peony	12
Protea	14
Rose	15
Sweet Pea	16
Zinnia	17

Living Gifts 19

African Violet	19
Aloe Vera	21
Amaryllis	22
Lemon Tree	23
Narcissus	24
Orchid	26
Additional Living Houseplants	28

PART 2: PERPETUAL POSIES & SITTING WITH SENTIMENTS 29

WHAT IS A POSY? 31

SENTIMENT GARDENS: PROVIDING NATURE'S TONIC 33

ON DESIGNING GARDENS 34

THE GARDENS AND THE POSIES 37

Celebrations 37
    The Celebrations Floriography Garden & Let's Celebrate Posy 38
    The Celebratory Sentiment Garden 40

Terms of Endearment 41
    The Terms of Endearment Floriography Garden & All About Love Posy ... 42
    The Love & Adoration Sentiment Garden 44

Health and Healing 45
    The Health & Healing Floriography Garden & Healing Wishes Posy 46
    The Healing and Restoration Sentiment Garden 48
    The Mental and Physical Gifts We Receive 49

Gratitude and Thanks......51
    The Gratitude and Thanks Floriography Garden and Thank-You Posy......52
    The Grateful Reflections Sentiment Garden......54

Prayer and Meditation......55
    The Faith and Resilience Floriography Garden and Faith and Resilience Posy......56
    The Prayer and Meditation Sentiment Garden......58

Bereavement and Loss......59
    The Bereavement and Loss Floriography Garden and Bereavement Posy......60
    The Sorrow and Grief Sentiment Garden......62

Friends and Flowers......63
    The Friends and Flowers Floriography Garden and Friendship Posy......64
    The Sentiments of Goodwill and Fellowship Garden......66

Empowerment and Ambition......67
    The Empowerment and Ambition Floriography Garden and Uniquely You Posy...68
    The Intent and Aspirations Sentiment Garden......70

PART 3: HOW TO ARRANGE POSIES AND BOUQUETS......73

GATHERING AND PREPARATION......75
Harvesting and Conditioning......75

METHODS AND INSTRUCTIONS......81
Posy Perfection and the Characteristics of Good Floral Design......81

Selecting Your Container......86

Ready, Set, Go!......88
    Tab-Style Ribbon Directions......92
    Layered, Double Bow–Style Ribbon Directions......94
    Sentiment Tags......97

Bountiful Bouquets......99
    Spiraled Tulips, Three Ways......99
    Soldiered Roses......106
    Sweet Peas, Posy-Style......109

PART 4: THE NEW LANGUAGE OF FLOWERS DICTIONARY (ABRIDGED) 113

THE NEW LANGUAGE OF FLOWERS 115

Essential Dictionary Notes 116

PART 5: QUICK-START DIRECTORIES 139

QUICK-START OCCASIONS DIRECTORY 141

Engagement 141

New Job or Career 141

Graduation 142

New Home or Living Environment 142

Childbirth 142

Achievements 143

End of Life 143

Illness and Injury 143

QUICK-START SENTIMENTS DIRECTORY 145

Fear 145

Pride 145

Joy 146

Troubled 146

Heartbreak 146

Excitement 147

Admiration 147

Confusion 148

RESOURCE DIRECTORY 149

Plants and Seeds 149

    PLANTS 150

    SEEDS 152

Plant Care and Gardening Tools 153

Gardening How-To and Plant Knowledge 153

Cut Flowers 154

UK-Based Directories 155
Materials and Methods Sources 156
Vases and Containers 157
Sentiment Tag Crafting Paper and Wrapping 158
Other Helpful Resources 159

BIBLIOGRAPHY 161
Book Sources 161
Internet Sources 162

Foreword

Heart forward and *flower forward* are phrases that come to mind when I think of Teresa Sabankaya. This has been true for the duration of my knowing of her work, and my knowing her through mutual garden and flower friends Lorene Edwards Forkner and Deb Prinzing, of the Slow Flowers Society. I knew of Teresa's work bringing the historic Language of Flowers into her floral design, specifically to animate people's relationship to their own flowers, whether those flowers were wild, food, medicine, culture, ritual, or beauty. I loved that concept!

And when I was gifted a copy of *The Posy Book: Garden Inspired Bouquets That Tell a Story*, my own imagination was animated as to the power and depth our garden flowers were additionally endowed with when—as Teresa invites us to do—narrative, story, and intentional expression were interwoven with them. She further lived into these ideas when in 2022, she generously opened her own home and garden to the Slow Flower's Summit speakers and included posies with encouraging messages for each of us. Such a gesture of common ground and kindness to a large and unknown group—who left that June evening as warm community.

Since she first opened her own heart and central California family land to a flower garden, she has—like the flowers themselves—shared them, their lessons, and their many gifts extravagantly forward with the world around her and far further afield. From her floral design studio tucked into her garden in Bonny Doon, California, to her books, including this one, to her online New Language of Flowers dictionary, to her lived life—Teresa gifts to us all her love of flowers, her belief in their ability to transform our lives and mindsets for the better, and their ability to help us express through flowers and our gardens and garden life stories the very best of what we want to communicate as caring humans—to one another and to the world.

When Teresa joined me on *Cultivating Place* as a guest in late 2020, she reminded us all through her posies and purpose of the enduring comfort of beautiful flowers, thoughtfulness, and kindness to transcend what might otherwise defeat us. It was a moment when we really needed these lessons, gifts, and reminders more than ever; I think we always need these reminders, don't you?

With that, enjoy this next of Teresa's heart-forward and flower-forward offerings! May the flowers and their ancient language that speaks to us all, but ever more clearly with Teresa's help in Modern Floriography, be with you always –

—JENNIFER JEWELL

Chico, CA

Jennifer Jewell is the creator and host of national, award-winning public radio program and podcast Cultivating Place: Conversations on Natural History and the Human Impulse to Garden. *Cultivatingplace.org*

INTRODUCTION
A Timely Revival

At her state funeral, the flowers that were placed atop the coffin of Her Majesty Queen Elizabeth were laden with connotations, sentiments, and symbolism. With intent, they were chosen to convey reverences of remembrance, love, beauty, gratitude, and much more. Within the flowers, herbs, and plants used in this composition, we witnessed a bestowing of great honor and respect for a mother and a queen through the language of flowers. This was a wonderful example of modern floriography.

For an exceptionally long time, flowers have been messengers of the heart. As far back as we can go to ancient Egypt, unearthed hieroglyphics featuring prominent references to trees, plants, and flowers prove a long-existing use in symbolism and notable meanings to humans. And since the fifteenth century, symbolic allusions to flowers, trees, plants, and herbs have graced the pages of some of our most important pieces of literature from around the world. Shakespeare, as an example, practiced extensive use of botanical references throughout his plays and sonnets. With nearly two hundred specific mentions of flowers, herbs, trees, seeds, spices, and many other varieties of flora, he provides us with some of the most memorable lines in literature to date. He is our world's greatest playwright, and he had an expansive awareness of botany with adeptness for using metaphors that connected our natural world to our literature and cultures.

But somewhere during the course of history, between the ancient Egyptian hieroglyphics to Shakespeare's literature to the present day, we have all but lost the delicate and splendorous use of our flowers and plants to signify and give depth and meaning to special moments, milestone events, and the countless, momentous feelings we perceive throughout our lives. This use and reference of flowers and plants throughout antiquity represents a yearning by our human spirit, and a simple outreach into another realm in nature to satiate our desire to experience feelings that aren't shallow and trivial. Contemplation about nature, and *in* nature, allow us to redirect inward to deeper knowledge, emotions, and thoughts. This is what this book's main purpose is: *To first acknowledge the use of flowers and plants to create messages and hold significant symbolism for us, and then how to use them in times of celebrations, milestones, daily anecdotes, and so much more.* We should consider the use of nature and flowers like this as our gifts because they truly are gifts—aesthetically, physiologically, and mentally—and they are demanding our deliciously slowed-down attention, poised and ready to guide us through our fast and furious pace of modern life.

When I began my business as a farmer-florist over twenty-five years ago, my aim was to reintroduce the lost art of creating and conveying messages with flowers, also known as *floriography*. I hoped that incorporating a language and message into floral designs would be a unique business model, and that proved to be true. I have learned that giving flowers crafted to tell a story is incredibly impactful and meaningful. So much more than just flowers, it is a chronicle in botanicals and gardens that lie in wait for us to unlock their vast, uplifting, and healing language.

I cannot wait for you to dig into this book, and I am so excited to share all that I know with you. Whether you are a professional in the trade, a novice flower lover, or a person simply curious and intrigued, you can use floriography in simple or elaborate ways to tell a story and receive messages from our gardens and flowers. I hope, with this book, you will gain an increased interest and understanding of the history and practice of this beautiful art form of floriography, and I also hope this book will ignite a longing to reconnect with nature and all its abundant gifts to us. And remember: Always be blooming!

How to Use This Book

This book is intended to imbue its readers with inspiration and impart knowledge in using the vast language and symbolism of flowers, plants, and gardens to convey messages to others—and collect the many sentiments they provide to us for our own well-being. I like to refer to these scores of messages and sentiments as *gifts from the garden*. In your practice of using them to convey messages and also receive them, you are engaging in floriography. It also means that you are well on your way to understanding the depths and impacts that floriography can provide you and whoever you choose to share it with.

This book provides you with simple tips on everything from planning a garden to cultivating and growing, buying and arranging flowers, creating live-plant gifts, and using all forms of botanical elements, from simple to elaborate offerings. You don't need a garden of your own to participate in floriography, and you will not require complicated training either. It gives me pure and unbridled joy to give away gifts from my garden, and that is what this book is about. To recognize the abundant and inspirational messages that our flowers and gardens convey to us, and then harness, embrace, and transform them into giving, sharing, and welcoming these beautiful endowments. I hope that this book remains in your reach for many years and becomes a multigenerational heirloom, and a favored source of knowledge and inspiration for you and your family.

In "Getting Acquainted with Floriography," I give explanations and provide pieces of history about the language of flowers. I also cover the modern version of creating messages with flowers and gardens in part 1, "Day-to-Day Floriography," which is a primary focus of this book. I will inspire creative ways to craft bouquets, unique arrangements, and potted live plants as messengers of the heart.

In part 2, "Perpetual Posies and Sitting with Sentiments," you will learn what a posy is, and I share eight intentional gardening plans with you, referred to as *Floriography Gardens*. These gardens are designed to provide you with the materials needed to create the subsequent posies that are featured, as well as their floral gifts. These gardens will provide you with ideas and inspiration, and coupled with their production of flowers for subsequent posies and bouquets, they are the cornerstone of this book. In addition to the flowers and plants used in each garden, there is also an alternate and seasonal variations list as well as cultivation instructions, care tips, and interesting facts that are found in each "Garden Notes" section.

Each garden also features its accompanying "Sentiment Garden" section, providing you with additional ideas and insight to create spaces that collect and provide the symbolisms and sentiments in a way that you can just sit and take in. The cutting gardens and sentiment gardens are certainly interchangeable, you can cut from either one, of course, and reflect the book's intent to demonstrate the multitude of ways that gardens can be used. Either way, I hope these garden plans and ideas provide you with refuge, enlightenment, and tranquility—because being in a place of nature, no matter the size or format, invites us to calibrate our souls and reset our hearts and minds.

In part 3, "How to Arrange Posies and Bouquets," I will teach the methods and techniques required to create stunning bouquets, and of course, you will learn how to create a perfectly harmonized posy that will tell a heartfelt story in the language of flowers. In using my simple guidelines and edifying tips, you will discover that you do not have to be an expert with endless skills to create stunningly beautiful gifts from your garden. It is a matter of being organized and prepared, and then applying the principles I will teach you here. I provide copious amounts of knowledge and expertise, which are the results of many years of experience in planning, growing, and designing with flowers and plants. To finish off your beautiful creations, we'll get into creative crafting with ribbons and sentiment tags, which is a charming, beautiful, and very necessary part of floriography. No offering of floriography is complete without them, as they are the only way the gift's secret messages and meanings are deciphered to its recipient. Without sentiment tags, they will be received as the beautiful botanical compilations they are but will not have the added depth and significance of the meanings, sentiments, and messages you would like to pass on to your recipient.

We will talk about the *sustainable approach* too, and how vital it is to incorporate earth-friendly practices in your gardening developments and floral designing methods and materials. Throughout this book, you will find several pull quotes called *Simply Sustainable*. These quotes share facts, ideas, and methods that make it easy to employ sustainability in your gardening and gifting practices. I do not look to sustainability as being a choice any longer. By adopting sustainability in all our practices and endeavors, we are assuring preservation of our valued resources, thus providing a brighter, cleaner, and healthier future for us all. Everything in this book can and should be done sustainably, and I will not only show you how but also provide you with numerous resources to make it attainable to you.

Part 4 covers "The New Language of Flowers Dictionary (Abridged)." This abbreviated dictionary is a springboard reference that offers a quick guide to a condensed list of readily available popular flowers and plants, along with their meanings. Also included are some newer entries for the more recent hybrid introductions. You will see many flowers and plants with their meanings sprinkled throughout the book, especially in part 2 among the descriptions of the floriography gardens and their subsequent posies as well as the sentiment gardens. In a plant's name and meaning, there will be botanical names, genera, species, variety if applicable, and also various symbols in these descriptions. See "Essential Dictionary Notes" in part 4 for a detailed description of the way plant names are written and what the symbols mean.

In my first published work, *The Posy Book*, you will find my original, comprehensive dictionary of the same name, which is a wonderful reference too. Ultimately, for the most complete and up-to-date compilation, a comprehensive lexicon is available online at **modernfloriography.com**. This website is continuously updated with new meanings for the latest hybridized flowers and plants and the addition of newly discovered meanings of flowers and plants that have been around for some time. I reference this site regularly and it has proven to be an incredible and handy resource when your books are not at hand.

Providing my readers with inspiration and guidance is essential—and I offer this in so many ways within this book—but resources can be overwhelming and knowing where to find the materials for creating all that I offer here is critical. For this reason, my *Resource Directory* is quite extensive. I have included sources that do not cater to the come-and-go fads and will provide hardy and long-lived connections that you can depend on for many years.

Disclaimer

In this book, I have incorporated suggestions for making herbal teas and referenced the medicinal attributes of various herbs and plants. But I am in no way offering medical advice nor suggesting or advising that you ingest, inhale, or put anything on your skin. Nor am I suggesting that you have any physical, mental, or physiological ailments. I am not a mental health or healthcare professional, rather, I am simply providing viewpoints and sharing results of my own research and experience on the connection between our overall well-being and nature.

Additionally, the illustrations in this book, which I have rendered myself, are not reflective of nor do they depict the scientific accuracy of botanicals. They are merely an artist's imaginative vision of gardens and plants.

GETTING ACQUAINTED WITH FLORIOGRAPHY

The word *floriography* may sound complicated, but it isn't. Floriography simply means *cryptologic communication through the use or arrangement of flowers*. It is an intricate and poetic form of communicating thoughts, emotions, and sentiments using trees, flowers, plants, and even entire gardens. Indeed, floriography refers to the language of flowers, but specifically, it is the intent to create a message or tell a story using the language of flowers. And when you put into practice using flowers and plants—as a messenger of your thoughts and sentiments—that makes you a floriographer.

Irrefutably, flowers and gardens have nurtured, provided for, healed, adorned us, given distinction and honor to heroes, commemorated life's various affairs and conveyed copious sentiments and messages—for thousands of years—in all cultures and in every part of the world. While exploring the history of flowers and their symbolic meanings, perhaps you will find it inspirational to know that by engaging in floriography today, you will tread on the heels of many cultures and emulate floral customs from numerous periods and eras in our history. To help you understand and appreciate the importance and powerful impact that flowers have held throughout the history of humanity, I have condensed and bulleted just a few of the most intriguing references to flowers and plants, their symbolisms, and practical uses of them.

ANCIENT EGYPT

❋ It is interesting to note that the lotus flowers Egyptians refer to in ancient texts and illustrations likely were not lotus but rather two genera of water lilies, the white water lily, *Nymphaea lotus*, and the blue water lily, *Nymphaea nouchali* var. *caerulea*. The lotus and water lily are two different plants with distinct characteristics and taxonomic classifications, but to keep confusion at bay, we refrain from referring to these flowers as "lily" when we talk or write about them in reference to ancient Egypt because they have always been referred to as the "lotus."

❋ The lotus is probably the most used and oldest form of floral art and symbolism we know. The Egyptians associated these flowers with their gods and, later, their kings. Ancient art and texts depict Tutankhamun as a reborn child, or sun god, rising from the petals of the sacred blue lotus.

Nymphaea nouchali var. *caerulea*, also known as the Egyptian lotus, blue water lily, sacred blue lily of the Nile, Cape water lily.

Hieroglyphic art in ancient tomb of Menna in Luxor, Egypt

- The blue lotus flower is the one considered most sacred. The flowers of the blue lotus close at night, retract themselves underwater, and then a new bloom will rise again the next morning and open fully to the sun. This process linked the blue lotus to the cycles of creation, death, and rebirth in the continuance of life.

- The white lotus blooms during the evening, which lent it to strong lunar associations in ancient Egypt and other cultures and eras.

- The lotus has been associated with health and healing, too, and its oil used medicinally as a cooling massage oil. It was employed to treat ailments of the liver, as well as in a bath to expel fever along with coriander.

- Flower heads of the lotus were soaked in wine to create a unique, intoxicating and fragrant drink for banquets and festivals, and the roots were ground into flour and used in other culinary dishes too.

- In temples, the lotus has been depicted in scenes being held to the nose of royalty by gods and goddesses, as its scent was considered restorative and protective.

- The oils of the lotus flower were extracted for perfumes and cosmetics such as lotions, and lip and cheek coloring. Early Egyptians invented the first perfume jar in the shape of the lotus to house the precious scented oil of its blooms, and in later years, the city of Alexandria became known as the perfume capital of the world, where each scent always began with the fragrant oil of the lotus flower.

- The lotus flower was commonly used as the principal element in floral collars that adorned the deceased, as it was believed the flowers protected the deceased from their enemies and ensured a safe passage to the next phase of their eternal journey.

ANCIENT GREECE AND ROME

- In Greek mythology, it was Chloris, the goddess of flowers, who made the first rose bloom by creating it from the lifeless body of a beautiful nymph she found in the forest. To make her eternal, Chloris transformed the beautiful nymph into a lovely rose. There are numerous flowers that were willed into existence by gods and goddesses in Greek mythology, and even today, we use some of the same symbolic meanings associated with their creations.

❀ In addition to the rose, which signifies *love* and *ephemeral beauty*, another example is the *Anemone*, or wind flower, that arose from the earth from the tears of the goddess Aphrodite when she found her lover Adonis dying from a wound caused by a wild boar. To this day, in the language of flowers, the *Anemone* signifies *abandonment* and *pain of parting*, among other things. The practice of commemorating the deceased with florals flowed into the Roman Empire, where elaborate displays of multiple flower types decorated the graves of their deceased ancestors, as well as recently departed loved ones.

❀ The great importance of flowers and plants in Roman culture is evident in their art, especially in mosaics and paintings. Virtually every statue created during this period contained flowers, leaves, or plants. Flora, the Roman goddess of flowers, is depicted in numerous variations of art throughout history, including paintings, sculptures, and statues. She is the absolute essence of flowers and our ongoing infatuation with their ephemeral beauty and perfection.

"Flora" – the Roman goddess of flowers. Terracotta. Ireland, circa 1810

From the New York Public Library, color lithograph by Walter Crane, Flora's feast: a masque of flowers. (London Cassell 1889) Crane, Walter (1845-1915), Author

❋ As the Romans adopted Greek myths, their poets wrote about the gods and goddesses and their earthly involvement with flowers. These are the first examples of literature and writings that depict flowers and plants as messengers—they hold the ability to connect the spirit worlds with reality. In other words, a connection between the realm of spirits and otherworldly gods and goddesses and 3D Earth with its flora and fauna.

MEDIEVAL TIMES

❋ In Medieval times, herbs and flowers were cultivated for medicinal use, as well as flavorings for food and drink. Additionally, a medieval garden often grew a considerable variety of botanicals intended for other uses like ornaments for clothing and hair as well as decorative elements such as wreaths and garlands.

Medical Herb Cultivation, 16th Century

INTRODUCTION: A TIMELY REVIVAL

❁ During this time in history, the bubonic plague killed some twenty million people in Europe. It was especially deadly in the larger towns and cities where it was impossible to prevent transmission from one person to another. They believed the plague and other diseases were spread by odor, thus, the posy and tussie-mussie (small bouquet) both originated by binding fragrant herbs and flowers together and hung from the neck or stuffed into pockets in hopes of warding off infectious disease.

A depiction of what a tussie or posy may have looked like during medieval times. The words 'tussie-mussie', or 'tusemose' is first mentioned in 1440, and is derived from the word tuse meaning knot of flowers, and mose referencing the damp moss that was wrapped around the stems to prevent the flowers from drying out. Included are the very fragrant herbs of rue, mint, sweet woodruff, chamomile, and rosemary.

Tacuinum Sanitatis, ca. 1400, Gathering sage
In addition to carrying herbs to ward off disease, strewing herbs were gathered and used to mask unpleasant smells & provide pest control inside homes. In medieval homes, floors were covered with rushes, reeds, and straw in order to cover the dirt earth, and provide insulation and bedding for sleeping. They also served to soak up spills and dropped food. However, these floor coverings were replaced only once or twice a year, so to thwart the accumulated odors, fragrant and astringent herbs were scattered—strewn--on top of them, which allowed releasing their scents when they were walked upon, disguising odors and deterring certain pests.

❋ Following the tussie-mussie and posy was the more elaborate nosegay, which was created to mask foul odors during a time when bathing was not a daily practice, and underground plumbing did not exist. The nosegay was useful in tucking up under the nose to offer a pleasant diversion from the horrendous odors found in highly populated areas.

A sample of Elizabethan nosegays. Nonsuch Palace by Joris Hoefnagel

RENAISSANCE PERIOD

❋ It was during the Renaissance era that flowers began to play an even more central role in the lives of people throughout Europe. There was a resurgence of art and culture during the Renaissance, and florals were highly regarded among both the aristocracy and commoners. Flowers heavily influenced the Renaissance-era painters, in whose works they were lavishly displayed, in all colors of the spectrum, typically flowing from urns, glass, silver, and terra-cotta.

❋ Gardening became a passion during this time, making flowers more readily available for everyday use, and not just for ceremonies or events. This is predominately the era in which the symbolism and language of flowers really gained momentum, and it became fashionable to use flowers as such, especially among the aristocracy.

> *A garden "shall contain the herbs and flowers used to make nosegays and garlands."*
> — THE COUNTRY FARME, 1600

INTRODUCTION: A TIMELY REVIVAL

VICTORIAN ERA

- Even though the Victorian era brought the language of flowers into popularity, we owe credit to the French for implementing a language associated with flowers in earlier times. One of the earliest language of flowers books ever published was *Abécédaire de Flore ou langage des fleurs* by B. Delachénaye, published in 1810. But the book, *Le langage des fleurs*, published in 1819 and written by Charlotte de la Latour (pseudonym of Louise Cortambert) proved to be the most prevalent book of its kind and was responsible for sparking the romantic idea of floriography, specifically poetry in flowers.

- Victorian England, while regrouping from a long war with France, was ready for symbolism and romance, and the people found the language of flowers incredibly charming and genius. It was a socially acceptable alternative way to communicate your innermost thoughts and ambitions—sentiments and secret messages could be conveyed to others without saying a word, and with beautiful flowers! The newfound art of floriography became so popular that it prompted the publishing of the sentimental language of flowers poems, books, social letters, and papers in abundance. This is what later became known as the "Victorian language of flowers phenomenon." More on the Victorian era and the history prior to it can be found in *The Posy Book*.

Literature, Playwrights, and Pre-Raphaelite Artworks

Throughout history, the most prolific uses of the language and symbolism of flowers, plants, and even gardens lie in literature and art. Following the Victorian era, a deviation in artwork from realism projected a loss of the expression and experience of nature and its language of symbolisms. This caused an uproar among some artists, which led to the formation of the Pre-Raphaelite Brotherhood, who denounced the art of the day. The Pre-Raphaelites championed the return of realism into artwork, and in particular the connection to nature and flowers. Their artwork was very refined and lifelike, and would recite tales and stories in elaborate detail, offering a *truth to nature* to the viewer. There are many wonderful examples of the Pre-Raphaelite influence, but one of the most prominent and well-known is Shakespeare's *Ophelia*.

Ophelia detail from a larger painting by Sir John Everett Millais (1829-1896), oil on canvas, 1851-2.

Shakespeare's writings and plays abound in floriography. The image of Ophelia, in the play *Hamlet*, as she prepares herself to drown in the river with garlands of blossoms is a prime example. Shakespeare deliberately chose specific flowers to convey the appropriate sentiments that Ophelia would carry with her to her death. It is readily apparent that these selections synchronized the messages and sentiments of death, mourning, resurrection, and innocence. The red poppy portrayed her looming death, the daisy represented her innocence, the buttercup reflected ingratitude, and the willow stood for sorrow and mourning—all accurately depicted the scene. Although Ophelia's drowning was not a pleasant event, it is a stellar example of the depth of meaning that flowers can convey.

MODERN HISTORY

It is pleasing to know that we have carried at least a small amount of some of these incredible parts of history forward into our modern times. You can find some annotations to the use of symbolism in flowers and plants in our literature, architecture, and other decorative items today, just as they were in use so long ago. For instance, the acanthus leaf, found on the columns of Greek temples beginning circa fifth century BCE, also decorate some of our present-day architecture. The acanthus symbolizes *the fine arts, enduring life, long life, rebirth, resurrection,* and *immortality*. On our modern-day buildings that are deemed significant in our cultural, political, and social structures, you will commonly see the acanthus leaf motif in the upper relief work, as well as on decorative corbels and columns. This hardy plant has especially ornate and beautiful leaves and thrives in less-than-ideal conditions worldwide. So, it is only fitting that it graces some of our most important structures and will continue to do so as time goes on.

Today, it is rare to witness the use of floriography when we give flowers or living botanical gifts to one another or incorporate the concept into our garden designs. This is such a shame because there are so many times in our lives when no words can convey our thoughts and feelings the way a beautiful bouquet, posy, or a living plant can. It is a timeless way, and it is practical and useful too. I believe we are ready to embrace things tried and true in our attempt to establish deeper meaning in an often-callous world.

PART 1
Day-to-Day Floriography

Agift from the garden tends to display physical and aesthetic beauty in the form of a floral bouquet, a pretty posy, or a gorgeous bunch of flowering cherry branches bound with satin ribbon. But it is also the often hidden and unrecognized gift of our emotional healing, and the desire and ability to disengage from the muddle of life's challenges. From the garden, we can acquire the remedies and energies needed to rejuvenate us. The gifts from our gardens are endless. And we've only just begun to discover the multitude of ways we can use these gifts.

I believe that when we create a posy, arrange a beautiful en masse bouquet, or dress up a living plant as gifts to others, it is therapeutic to both the giver and receiver. Whether you are gathering your own garden-grown materials or buying a bouquet or grower bunch of flowers from the grocery store—or a mixture of both—it does wonders for your heart and soul to create something so beautiful with natural, living elements such as flowers and living plants. These make stunningly beautiful botanical gifts that are guaranteed to be well received and admired as a memorable gesture for years to come.

> *I work at my garden all the time and with love.*
> *What I need most are flowers, always.*
> —Claude Monet (1840–1926)

En Masse
Bouquets

The word *monobotanical* defines a bouquet or arrangement of flowers that are all of one type, such as tulips, or a vase full of multicolored roses. Another interchangeable term we can use is *en masse*, meaning "*all together, as a group*, and *collectively.*" In this book, I use the term *en masse*, and always of the monobotanical definition, meaning of "*all one type* of plant material." The en masse style creates the opportunity to appreciate the flowers' complexity while highlighting their structure, color, and extraordinary beauty. We can learn to admire flowers in a different way using this style, and as a florist for many years, I have used this style abundantly, and always with astonishing results. It is a simple aesthetic that can be spruced up to a very elegant presentation or left in a simple and organic array. Because the en masse style is just one type of flower, it is usually a very quick and easy compilation to create, and you won't need an assortment of different blooms from the garden, only a few—or a lot— of your preferred flower. Additionally, the sentiment tag that you will attach to your gift leaves much room for creativity because you'll have only one flower to decipher. Sentiment tags and their vital role in floriography are discussed in detail later, in part 3.

In the following several pages, I share with you some of my favorite blooms gathered in their seasonal prime—actually, I'll bet most of them are pretty much everyone's garden favorites, and that's always the best, in my opinion, because they evoke a sense of *place* and draw you closer to people and locales with their familiarity and associations. Some of the florals featured here may be tricky to source, but try not to select them when outside of their natural growing cycle—and especially don't defer to imported flowers or highly commercialized and altered states of a bloom. Always try to remember that floral gifts should trigger connection and belongingness along with their beauty. That, coupled with a respectful nod to nature and sustainability, makes for a presentation that reminds one of a beautiful garden that will always dazzle and captivate its recipient.

BABY'S BREATH

Gypsophila, or baby's breath, derived its name from the soil type it thrives in, which is high in gypsum, a kind of mineral that makes the soil thick and heavy. Contrary to the soil conditions it loves, baby's breath is the epitome of light and air and is readily available for use in everyday floriography. It wasn't that long ago that baby's breath held a bad reputation in the floral industry—and it is no wonder, considering that reduced or eliminated tariffs allowed floral wholesalers to import them from Mexico and South America in high volumes at low prices. Therefore, our market was literally flooded with baby's breath for many years, resulting in an almost sickening overuse of it. Thankfully, this sweet flower is slowly on the upswing again, because when used correctly, they are a very beautiful, whimsical addition to en masse arrangements and posies as well.

SIMPLY *Sustainable*

If you are acquiring your cut flowers outside your own garden, please purchase locally grown, grown in your region of your state, grown within your state, or grown somewhere in your country—and in this order. More information and sources for local cut flowers can be found in the *Resource Directory,* under "Cut Flowers."

As a gift to a newlywed couple, baby's breath, placed into a lovely cut crystal vase is adorned with a simple sentiment tag to decode its message. Baby's breath can be elegant in the en masse style, where it's the shining star in a display of **everlasting love, innocence, modesty, sweet beauty, purity of heart**, and ***festivity***.

> "For various reasons, be it economic, trade, or government policy, the floral industry since the early 1990s has undergone a major shift in the way flowers are grown and marketed. Slow Flowers™ began in the U.S., where 80 percent of cut flowers sold are imported from other countries and continents. The movement recognizes that this is not sustainable for people or for the planet, particularly when flowers are often considered a luxury. Slow Flowers believes that it is irresponsible to support the continued production and consumption of a perishable product that devours so many valuable resources (jet fuel, packaging material, water, to name a few), especially when there is a domestic alternative to imported flowers."
>
> —*From the Slow Flowers Manifesto, SlowFlowers.com*

CALLA LILY

In the language of flowers, the calla lily, *Zantedeschia aethiopica*, are substantial carriers of **love** and **beauty** sentiments with a dose of **charm** and **strength**. Other common names for callas include arum lily, Easter lily, lily of the Nile, and trumpet lily, and the mini-callas are included in this group as well. They have a unique slim and elegant chalice shape, and that, coupled with their extraordinary opaque coloring, is what makes them a stunner of a flower. A sampling of the calla lily's extraordinary sentiments includes **beauty**

A Calla-Card, as featured here, is a fun and unique way to present your gift of floriography with mini-callas. It is suitable for them because they are quite self-sustaining when out of water and will last and stay fresh for several hours like this. There are many other flowers that will adhere to this style as well. Some examples are *Chrysanthemums* (not spider varieties, as the petals will flop), statice, *Proteas*, and orchid blooms.

DAY-TO-DAY FLORIOGRAPHY: EN MASSE BOUQUETS

and loveliness, maiden modesty, pure elegance, magnificent beauty, delicacy, overcoming your challenges, panache, ardor, transition and growth, rebirth, and resurrection. Because they are messengers of such beauty and spirit, they are an appropriate gift for many occasions. And they carry secondary meanings according to their colors, just as a rose does, signifying each color's separate meaning in the language of flowers.

To grow your own calla lilies, you'll need to offer them a spot that receives at least six hours or more of sun. The plants need adequate light to bloom, so full shade is not recommended. They do not like dry soil and require steadily moist soil with heavy fertilization. And rodents such as squirrels and gophers and mammals such as moles love them, so for this reason, as well as the moisture requirements, I recommend growing them in containers.

How TO CREATE YOUR OWN *Calla-Card*

MATERIALS

- Card-stock paper, 110 lb or heavier
- 3 stems of mini-callas
- X-Acto knife or box cutter
- Green florists tape, ½" wide
- Clear tape

METHOD

Create a Word document with the name and meanings you'd like to use, as well as placing the hint "In the Language of Flowers" somewhere on the card, which will signal to the recipient that there is a coded message for them. Be sure to leave open space in the center, horizontally and vertically, for you to place the stem band. Print it out on heavy card stock in the color of your choice. Alternatively, you don't need to use Word, as a handwritten card is absolutely a beautiful and impactful way of personalizing your gift.

Cut out the card to a size of approximately 4 x 6" and set on a surface suitable for using an X-Acto knife or box cutter tool.

Create a band for the stems in the middle of the card by making two horizontal slits no more than 1" long across the paper, and about 1" apart from each other.

Cut the stems down on the flowers to approximately 2" long. Bind your callas together in a pleasing fashion with florists' stem tape and then slide them down behind the slit in the card, and then back through to the front, resting the bottom of the stems on the front side of your card. For additional stability, and for them to stay better in place, you can use clear tape across the stems on the backside of the card.

COSMOS

I believe such a fun and unique flower calls for an artistic pottery vase. And here, the chocolate cosmo is appreciated en masse in their various states of bloom life. This gift not only smells heavenly but also presents a quirky yet elegant aesthetic. Source for the vase can be found in the *Resource Directory*.

In the language of flowers, the cosmo, *Cosmos bipinnatus*, conveys a cornucopia of sentiments and symbolism—**modesty, pure love of a virgin, innocent beauty, universal love around the world, balance, come walk with me, harmony, modesty, orderly, peacefulness,** and *tranquility*—and that's just a few! But the chocolate cosmo is in a world of its own with its secondary meanings of **simple pleasures**, and **deepest love for you**. They are a luxury in the garden, where no other flower can compete with its exotic chocolate scent and velvety, dark, confection-like petals. Imagine all that delectable beauty in a sweet vase or wrapped posy-style in beautiful tissue.

It's easy to grow chocolate cosmos in your garden or in pots on the patio. You will need at least six hours of direct sun daily, coupled with moderate but deep watering, and an occasional feeding with flower fertilizer. They are native to Mexico, so you'll need to dig up the tubers and store over the cold season in temperature zones of 50°F or below. Trust me when I say that once you've grown these beauties, your garden will never be complete without them!

DAFFODIL

Daffodils, a common name for the genus *Narcissus,* signal a long-awaited spring each year and blanket our gardens, hillsides, and forest glens with their nodding heads, bright and sunny colors, and sweet fragrance. Daffodils belong to the very large and diverse Amaryllidaceae family that includes hundreds of different species, varieties, and forms. The American Daffodil Society has established thirteen separate divisions of daffodils, which includes hundreds of different varieties within each of those divisions. We have come a very long way since the earliest days of the big yellow old-fashioned *jonquils*. And because of this, their meanings and interpretations in the language of flowers can be somewhat intricate and mystifying. I recommend focusing on a few of the primary symbolisms and meanings of the daffodil, which are varied enough that they can be used for many different occasions and sentiments. Here are just a few: ***regard, respect, unrequited love, sunshine, the sun shines when I am with you, high regards, honesty, respect,*** and ***simple pleasures***. Once you've familiarized yourself with the primary meanings, and if you

When gifted as a bunch, daffodils represent *joy, happiness*, and *celebration*. The abundant colors and patterns available in gift tissue makes it difficult to select your favorite. Here, I think the color of the tissue reflects the cheerful feel of the sentiment and the season of the flowers perfectly.

feel inclined to explore deeper into their secondary meanings, according to colors, the way they are presented to another, and of course, various forms, cultivars, and varieties, then browse the online reference of this book at **modernfloriography.com.**

Daffodils are spring-blooming bulbs and are incredibly rewarding to grow. They offer such a big show and are very forgiving if circumstances aren't optimal for them. Grown in the ground or in pots, their only true requirements are a winter chill, and at least six hours of full sun during the spring and summer months. If you live in a temperate or subtropical climate, you might have to dig them up, store them in a dark, cool area, and replant them in the spring to afford them the required chilling period.

In the language of flowers, the Dahlia is infused with layers of meanings. As seen here, a vase arrangement of *Dahlias*, regardless of their color, conveys messages of **dignity, eloquence, instability, forever yours, refinement, novelty, elegance,** and **gratitude**.

DAHLIA

Dahlias were discovered in the sixteenth century by Spanish botanists, who noted them growing wild on the hillsides in Mexico. They were one of the first plants to be introduced to Europe and were originally grown as food crop for their edible tubers. Today, there are few home gardens that are without a *Dahlia* or two. There are over thirty species and over twenty thousand cultivars with blooms that are varied in size, shapes, and colors to choose from, so surely there is a right *Dahlia* for every garden. *Dahlias* are not that difficult to grow, and the reward is their showstopping blooms from summer to fall. Additionally, some varieties have dark foliage that, along with the flowers, lend considerable beauty and elegance to the garden. They are cold hardy down to 20°F, so if you are in a climate where outdoor temperatures normally drop below that, consider growing them in pots so that you can move them to a protected climate during cold temperatures. If your climate gets near the low of 20°F, but not for frequent and long periods, you can overwinter them in the ground by adding a thick layer of mulch before the cold season. Before mulching, and after the plant is spent during late fall, cut the stems back approximately three inches from the tuber to remove all the dead stems and foliage in preparation for mulching.

It is important, whether in pots or planted in the ground, that they have good drainage and regular watering throughout the summer months, especially if it is hot and dry.

HELLEBORE

The perfection of a *Helleborus* bloom is incomparable with any other flower, as it should be, because they are quite unique in their composition. The petals of a hellebore are very short, often unnoticed, and in some cases, almost invisible. It is the outer, larger, colorful sepals, not petals, that we find stunningly beautiful. Some come with sporadic spotting, some with artful swaths of coordinating shades, and some are a solid, opaque hue. The sepals are formed around the flowers for protection from harsh winter elements, allowing them to bloom even then! And this is why the hellebore blooms face downward.

Nature has designed the perfect umbrella for them to sustain themselves through snow and rain. They are anecdotic in their beauty, sometimes portraying complex, ruffled sepal formation and other times a very simple and elegant layout. In either case, I believe it's their central apex formation and anthers that are entrancing, hence a couple of their meanings in the language of flowers, **serenity** and **tranquility**.

Hellebores are grown without much fuss and will tolerate a host of climates. There is nothing else in the winter garden as beautiful, in my opinion, and such a welcome sight. The foliage of the plant remains green all year long too, which makes them even more accommodating in the garden scene. They are extremely low maintenance, and the only

Can you imagine receiving this bundle of beauty? Those smiling faces, the papers, the ribbon cohesively complementing the outer edges of those frilly petals. And with the sentiments of **relieves anxiety, protection against calumny,** and ***a beautiful year ahead***, it's no wonder this gift will rank superior!

MODERN FLORIOGRAPHY

things they are temperamental about are their planting locations, and their absolute resentment of being dug up and moved. Before you plant them, think about their native habitat—woodland bogs. Plant them in a spot where they will have regular moisture, but not bog-level moisture, and not too much sun. Plant in the right place the first time for the best success and joy for many years to come.

LADY'S MANTLE

Lady's mantle, *Alchemilla mollis*, is such a lovely messenger of a sentiment that is perfect for so many reasons—**comforting love**—which makes them a worthwhile addition to a garden or even a potted display just so you can make use of their charming sentiment. Their airy and whimsical blooms are rather magical when gathered en masse as a gift to others, but the leaves are the most interesting characteristic of the plant, both in and out of the garden. They are soft, velvety green and resemble crinkled dessert plates or petticoats that pinwheel toward the center and top of its stem, providing a resting place for the morning dew or rain to collect. This ability to capture morning dew gave them much historical folklore as being magic and spellbinding. Their Latin name, *Alchemilla,* is

With the sentiment of ***comforting love***, the soft and velvety leaves of lady's mantle, along with their rich, chartreuse blooms, made me feel that I did not want to conceal them with any wrapping at all in this arrangement. And this is the case sometimes, as it is utterly charming and lovely to leave the flowers in an undressed and unfussed state. But even so, a sentiment tag must be included with the bunch, otherwise your recipient will not be able to translate your gesture of a heartfelt sentiment to them.

related to *alchemy*, which also means "magic and sorcery," and it was believed the dew collected from their leaves held the essence of the celestial fire within the earth, therefore making an outstanding and revered form of water for use in alchemical processes. The moisture pooled on their leaves looks simply spellbinding and beautiful, as though you're looking to eternity through perfectly round pieces of glass, and it was believed that if you held your gaze long enough, then the little puddles of water would turn to diamonds! Lady's mantle has long been a symbol of purity, too, as its cloak-like leaves were thought to resemble the Virgin Mary's mantle, connecting it to notions of **womanhood** and **sanctity**.

Lady's mantle is simple to grow and will be happy in shade as well as full-sun locations. It does prefer a bit of acidity in the soil and will thrive in most temperatures, but in hot climates, it prefers some shade. They are charming when planted in masses under oaks, rambling through borders, and lining walks. If the allure of the lady's mantle has prompted you to grow this prolific, reseeding perennial plant in your own garden, avoid overspread by removing the spent flowers prior to setting their seeds.

PEONY

The peony, *Paeonia officinalis*, is a highly regarded and much-adored plant worldwide. It has been cultivated in Asia for centuries and has been shrouded with symbolism and folklore for just as long. There are few flowers as ornate, complex, and simply gorgeous as a peony, and because of this, they have been the subject of paintings, carvings, and an abundant number of decorative touches worldwide, and in all cultures. Their luxurious and spectacular beauty, combined with their hardiness and endurance in the garden, ushers our greatest respect and admiration for them.

Nothing tops a vase arrangement of these exquisite peony blooms for a gift of *compassion*. This gift is perfect for when you need to keep the blooms hydrated for a longer time or want to elevate the gift to a more formal presentation.

The soft petals of the peony remind us of comfort and contentment while their voluptuousness is a thrill of luxury and refinement. This pretty presentation is enhanced by coordinating paper, tissue, and ribbons, and the sentiment tag is matched to perfection with a message of ***happy marriage, happy life***.

These are a few of the reasons that the peony holds extensive meanings and symbolism in the language of flowers—***hands full of cash, welcome, happy marriage and happy life, aphrodisiac, hardiness, bashfulness, riches and honor, romance, bravery***, and more.

Peonies are one of the most highly anticipated and rewarding flowers to grow in your garden too. But there is one caveat—in order to bloom efficiently, peonies require a winter dormancy period of about six weeks, with the temperature consistently at about 40°F or lower. This means that if you live in a warm climate with milder winters, while you may be able to keep one alive, you may never see your peony bloom—and if it does bloom for you, it may be a very small bloom and not as robust as it would be if it were grown in a colder climate that fulfills its cold weather needs. However, from my own experience, the new hybrid varieties, such as the Itoh peony, which is a cross between the herbaceous peony (as featured in these photos) and a tree peony, require less time in a consistently cold dormancy to bloom. And, in the language of flowers, the entire genera hold the same meanings. At least for now!

DAY-TO-DAY FLORIOGRAPHY: EN MASSE BOUQUETS

PROTEA

The *Protea* has gained popularity in home gardens and as luxurious cut flowers in recent years, and in the language of flowers, they carry primary meanings of **steadfastness, diversity, loyalty,** and **intent**. There have been additional secondary meanings attached to the different varieties in the family of Proteaceae, which is comprised of eighty genera and over seventeen hundred species. For example, *Protea cynaroides*, commonly known as king protea, has taken its own symbolism and meaning in the language of flowers as **courage**, and the genus *Grevillea,* now has its own sentiments of **impulsive acts of love** and **elope with me**. And because of my own love for the popular woolly bush, *Adenanthos sericeu*s, also in the Proteaceae family, I have attached the new meanings, **tenacious but subdued, gentleness, tolerance,** and **forgiving** to it. It is appropriate to use the meaning of your choosing for all genera of *Protea*, whether it is the primary or secondary, or a mixture of both, as they are equally attached to the flower.

Growing any variety of *Protea* can be either a challenge or a walk on easy street, and this depends on your growing climate. *Proteas* are primarily native to South Africa, with some genera from Australia. They must have full sun, good air movement around the plant, and excellent drainage. They will struggle and most likely not survive in climates

Featured here, the *Protea* 'Pink Ice' conveys its lovely sentiments of **steadfastness, loyalty, diversity**, and **intent** to an admired friend. The market-style wrap in kraft paper is perfect for thick, sturdy-stemmed flowers like *Protea*, as the paper is strong enough to secure and hold the stems in place, yet soft enough not to damage blooms and blossoms.

that reach lows of 25 to 30°F. So, in essence, they will not survive outside USDA zones 9–12, leaving those in these other climates to enjoy their blooms as procured cut flowers rather than growing them in the garden. See the *Resource Directory* for more information on obtaining both cut flowers and protea plants and seeds.

Whether or not you've grown them, the Proteaceae family of spectacular flowers make a perfect choice for a gift in case of healing in loss, or for any type of accomplishment such as a graduation, a new career, and even a surprise marriage! So many milestones and occasions can be honored with this group of flowers, and new and more specific sentiments and meanings will certainly develop in the future.

Nothing says love like a rose . . . they are the **ambassadors of love**! Seen here wrapped in newsprint decoupage paper and tied with ribbon, this gift is an unforgettable offering of true love. These garden roses are also known as the cabbage rose, and because of their stem's natural pliability and often untethered nature, look stunning when presented in a staircase style. To achieve this, simply lay one rose at the top of your paper, and then lay them staggered down, in an alternating method—one side, then the other, until they are laying softly woven in and out of one another. Bind them just below the bottom of the last bloom laid, and finish with ribbon and sentiment tag. For an additional rose wrapping and presentation style, see part 3, under "Bountiful Bouquets."

ROSE

There is no other flower that symbolizes so much as *Rosa L.,* the world-renowned rose. For millennia, roses have captured our hearts in every way, from their stunning and unparalleled beauty and fragrance to their remarkable adaptability in varied and numerous climates. Contrary to what most people believe, roses are amazingly easy to grow, and there are roses that have been hybridized and set to grow in virtually every environment. So, it does not matter where you live, if you have a garden, patio, or a three-by-three-foot balcony in a high-rise building, you can grow a rose! And in the language of flowers, there are copious messages and sentiments that a rose can impart.

Using some of its primary meanings, a rose is the absolute perfect conveyor of *love, friendship, honor, beauty, congratulations,* and *grace.* To explore the many additional meanings of the rose, depending upon colors, varieties, and even how you present them to another, check out **modernfloriography.com,** and start your own love affair with this centuries old flower.

SWEET PEA

Sweet peas are a longtime favorite of many people. Their ethereal flowers evoke timelessness and memories for many people, and almost everyone's grandmother grew sweet peas. They imply numerous meanings in the language of flowers, and their dainty, ruffled petals and renowned sweet fragrance become an irresistible ball of love and infatuation when drawn together en masse.

Sweet peas can easily be grown from seed, and once they've reached a height of six or seven inches, they love to be set out into cool spring temperatures. They will need a trellis or other structure to ramble and climb on, and how large would depend on the variety you grow. Some are quite petite and will look lovely simply spilling from a pot, and some need a long fence line or long trellis to travel on. Either way, I am a firm believer that every person should grow a sweet pea or two at least once in their lifetime.

Here, a delicate nosegay of sweet peas placed inside a silver goblet makes a memorable gift to convey the sentiments of ***thank you for a lovely time!***

The meaning, ***delicate pleasures***, is conveyed in this market-style wrapped bouquet of sweet peas and proves the diversity of this flower is endless! This sentiment is a perfect reminder of the simple pleasures in life and the joy of every day.

See part 3, under "Bountiful Bouquets," for an additional wrapping style and sentiment theme for sweet peas.

ZINNIA

If there were a perfect plant to teach one how to save seed, plant seed, watch it grow, cut copious amounts of flowers, then repeat, it would be the *Zinnia elegans*. It is one of the most common garden flowers, easy to grow, and grown by so many and for so many years. For most people, a garden without a *Zinnia* is barely complete. *Zinnias* offer a lot of bang for the buck, and with very little input. You can sow the seeds directly into the ground after your last frost—in fact, they prefer that rather than transplanting. And they'll need 6 to 8 hours of sun and plenty of air circulation around them due to their tendency to harbor foliar diseases such as powdery mildew. I can't think of any other flower that adds such vibrant, steady color from summer through fall than this lively and steadfast garden flower. And in the language of flowers, their representation of **kind thoughts of absent friends**, or **absence**, makes them useful when you need convey this to a friend, or it's also nice to just take a seat in a patch of *Zinnias* and think of people that you miss.

Here is a lovely presentation of sumptuous *Zinnias* wrapped in beautiful tissue and tulle, which can be presented to a friend (or lover!) for a spectacular way to tell them, ***I miss you!***

DAY-TO-DAY FLORIOGRAPHY: EN MASSE BOUQUETS

Living
Gifts

Living plants are gifts that keep giving for many years, truly, and in some cases will be handed down through generations if they are well cared for. Here, I am including only a few samples of the vast array of potted plants that can be jazzed up, decorated, and given away as a gift. And their messages and symbolisms in floriography are astounding, diverse, and copious. In addition to these featured here, please see part 4, "The New Language of Flowers Dictionary (Abridged)," as I have included several popular and easily attainable living plants that would be appropriate for floriography gifts.

AFRICAN VIOLET

African violets, *Saintpaulia*, represent ***faithfulness*** and ***devotion***, and they make brilliant gifts to parents, children, aunts, uncles, colleagues, and friends. Because of the ***faithfulness*** and ***devotion*** theme, they can be used in many variations of a message in the language of flowers. This is one gift that will just keep giving as they are so long-lived, and with proper care, that's up to fifty years! They are compact, so they do not need a lot of space, and they are one of the only houseplants that will give you beautiful flowers almost year-round.

African violets evoke delightful memories because usually, your grandmother, aunt, or other relative had an African violet (or more, in my case!) growing in their house. They are a simple and beautiful joy to have around, especially in the dead of a long cold winter. Imagine these cheerful blooms uplifting you on a cold, gray day! African violets are easy to propagate into more plants, another aspect which makes them fun to receive and rewarding to grow. That's what we do in my family, we propagate them and grow them into new and beautiful plants to share among us all. I keep a substantial collection of violets, and they were a favorite of my dear late mother. In fact, I have had her violets in my safekeeping for several years now since her passing, and nothing warms my heart more than walking by my violets and thinking of her and how she just adored them.

What a pretty, unique, and cherished gift for a newly-wed couple this violet presentation makes. A stunning, white-blooming violet gets dressed up by tucking pretty tissue into a vintage candy dish, then winding a decorative pearl strand through the dainty blooms, which adds a bit of formality, resulting in an exquisite gift for the couple.

Where else would one find a charming gift for a devoted friend such as this sweetness? A miniature violet set into a vintage teacup is literally the epitome of perfection and will remain a treasured keepsake—both the teacup and the violet—for many years to come.

Contrary to what you see often in photo styling and sometimes even marketed in larger chain stores' garden departments, African violets do not live happily in terrariums. While they do love humidity, they are subject to root rot, so constant moisture inside terrariums is a sure bet they will not survive, or at least struggle greatly with spotted, weak, and floppy leaves. African violets like bright, indirect light, much like an orchid. Set them approximately 2 feet back from windows, and preferably in a south-southwest-facing direction. Never set them in full sun, as doing so will burn the leaves. Water with lukewarm water all around the edge of the plant, careful not to get water in the crown of the plant or leaves. The wicking method of watering is beneficial if you are not the best at regulating their moisture content and water needs yourself. The wicking method provides moisture from the wick to the soil as needed, and can also provide humidity, which they love. Although I water from the top, during particularly dry seasons I will set them all in saucers of water for about 30 minutes to send up the much-needed humidity. For a houseplant that is continuously growing and blooming, regular feeding is critical. Feeding once monthly with an organic liquid African violet food is beneficial for their health and longevity. For more information on the care and procurement of African violets, see the African Violet Society of America website at **africanvioletsocietyof america.org**.

ALOE VERA

Did you know that growing *Aloe vera* as houseplants will protect against household accidents and maliciousness? For that reason alone, they would make wonderful

Potting up a beautiful *Aloe vera* can be a bit hazardous, so be sure to use protective gloves and clothing to protect yourself from their thorns. *Aloe vera* is an appropriate offering for so many occasions, but here I have used the sentiments of ***good luck*** and ***protection*** that makes it a befitting college send-off gift.

housewarming gifts—and what about one for you too? The *Aloe vera* has been associated with sentiments of ***healing*** and ***luck*** since ancient times, and today they are closely associated with ***health***, as they are a most effective healer because of their antioxidant and antibacterial properties. ***Wisdom, integrity, luck, religious superstition, small talk,*** and ***sorrow*** are a few more of the meanings attached to this incredible, historic plant.

Aloe vera as a houseplant requires very little care. They will need a succulent soil mix, a sunny south- or southwest-facing window, and a bit of watering. Do let them dry out between watering, and if you see mushy leaves, you're overwatering. If you see browned leaf tips, then you're underwatering.

AMARYLLIS

Amaryllis, the common name for this ornamental cultivar of the genus *Hippeastrum,* is a tender perennial bulb that has become wildly popular when forcing bulbs for use in gifting and decoration during the holidays. Their large and lush, trumpetlike blooms can last up to seven weeks indoors, bringing unbridled joy, colors, and a truly marvelous scene to our indoor winter decorations. They are such showstoppers in bloom that they often need no more than a simple cachepot to set them in to admire their long, strappy leaves coupled with enormous, luminous flower heads. Forcing your amaryllis bulb

The stunning amaryllis and their adoring messages of **pride, splendid beauty,** and **timidity** make an exquisite bestowal to a cherished person in your life, and for many occasions. Once the blooms have faded, the bulb, with proper care, will rebloom yearly for a gift that never ceases to amaze. When gifting an amaryllis or any other higher maintenance or unusual plant to someone, it's always good to include a care guide. That way you don't burden the recipient with how do I take care of this? See the *Resource Directory* for websites that offer growing and care instructions. You can easily print out the care tips or handwrite them to include with your gifts.

into bloom is easy enough to do; just follow the directions that come with your bulb.

In their natural, unforced environment, an amaryllis would bloom in spring and summer in the garden. It's fun to grow them in their natural environment if you live in the required climate, which is USDA zones 8–10. And what an exciting achievement to see such a spectacular flower pop up every year, and that can be many years, as the amaryllis bulb can live up to seventy-five years!

LEMON TREE

Growing lemon trees in pots is easier than one might think and allows you to control their environment, which oftentimes creates a healthier, more robust tree than if it were in the ground in its ideal climate. So, don't shy away from growing lemons in pots! They will need 6–8 hours of sunlight daily, continuously

Often, we want to express our care and thoughts to someone who is ill but are not sure of how to do it. Yes, a greeting card is nice, and doing errands or special chores to help them out is always a good idea as well. But imagine the impact, the longtime appreciation they will feel when gifted with a living thing that will always remind them of your thoughtful gesture and message of *healing* and *health*.

moist soil but not soggy, and regular feeding with a citrus-specific plant fertilizer throughout the growing season, which is from late summer through approximately April. You can learn more about growing citrus in pots by reviewing some of the gardening sites I recommend in the *Resource Directory*.

NARCISSUS

Narcissus papyraceus is a perennial bulb variety in the very large genus of *Narcissus* and are specifically classified as *tazetta* within the genus. As noted earlier in "En Masse Bouquets," daffodils are also part of the same genus, and to simplify, *Narcissus* are daffodils, and daffodils are *Narcissus*! They are synonymous, and *Narcissus* is the Latin or botanical name for all daffodils, and daffodil is the common name of all members in the genus *Narcissus*. Now that we've got that out of the way, let's talk about the highly popular variety of daffodils called paperwhite *Narcissus*. There is hardly a home during the holidays that does not have at least one tray or vase with these symbolic and stalwart blooms creating festive and prominent displays throughout. They are absolutely the simplest bulb to force indoors, and that alone is highly rewarding. But when you learn and use all their meanings in the language of flowers, I believe that they would become even more popular—if that's even possible, and not just for the holidays either. Heartwarming sentiments such as **hope and renewal, sweetness**, and **you are sweet**, among other things, make them appropriate for recovery from illness, a birthday, and much more.

There are numerous varieties of paperwhites, all of which can be distinguished from other daffodils by their flowering characteristics, which usually

Here, the *Narcissus* variety 'Ziva' delights with their delightfully flowered heads. Planted in terra-cotta, the setting is rustic, yet elegant while conveying the tender messages of **stay as sweet as you are,** and **you're the only one**.

24 MODERN FLORIOGRAPHY

appear in clusters of 3 to 20 flowers to a stem, and almost always fragrant. Some smell sweet, others not so sweet, but more of a musky fragrance that you either love or don't. If you do not love the traditional paperwhite fragrance, choose the varieties that have the sweeter scent, which tend to be the more modern hybrid cultivars such as 'Ziva' or 'Nir.'

When growing *Narcissus*, you will need to grow the bulbs in a room with temperatures between 50 and 60°F. Make sure they get lots of bright, indirect light once they've sprouted, but keep the bulbs away from hot sun and heat to extend the bloom time. Usually, these protocols will keep your stems a bit stockier and not too leggy, but you will most likely still need to support the blooms so they don't sway and fall over. I suggest doing this the nature-led way, by selecting branches that have fallen to the ground along with mosses, lichen—even a few acorns to set a beautiful and natural scene around the plants and for the indoor environment where you'll place them.

Here is the seemingly timeless classic paperwhite *Narcissus* all dressed up for a holiday showpiece or gift. Using the variety "Ariel" here for another well-endowed bloom count atop sturdy stems, this variety carries a bit more old-fashioned *Narcissus* fragrance, being less sweet than 'Ziva.' Blooming paperwhites evoke a lovely winter's scene, complete with dainty flowers akin to flurries of snow and shimmering snowflakes, which is what makes them such a popular decorative plant and gift through the winter holidays. And the beautifully crafted sentiment tag attached to the display conveys **hope, renewal, prosperity,** and ***gracefulness***, which adds such a heartfelt enrichment to the winter holidays and into the New Year.

SIMPLY *Sustainable*

Peat moss is ancient plant matter from peat bogs, which are delicate wetland ecosystems. Peat is a nonrenewable resource because it takes many years to form and reduces our available wetlands and, in turn, alters these ecosystems negatively. There are processes underway that would ease impact on the growing and harvesting of peat, but until then, we must restrict the depletion and taxing of the environment.

In our endeavors to create beautiful botanical presentations, peat moss certainly can be replaced with other sustainable products. Rice hulls, pine tree needles, coconut husk chips and coir, and tree bark are just a few options. See the *Resource Directory* for where to obtain sustainable alternatives for peat.

ORCHID

The orchid family, Orchidaceae, is the largest flowering plant family on earth, with about twenty-eight thousand species. It is also one of the oldest, having developed about 100 to 125 million years ago, which means that orchids are as old as the dinosaurs! This is why, in Asian traditions, the orchid symbolizes **strength** and **endurance**. In all my many years as a florist, I have never met anyone who does not love orchids. I have, however, met people who are intimidated at, and cringe at the thought of growing them, or trying to—but regardless, we all tend to have a love affair with these gorgeous, exotic, tremendously industrious plants. In the language of flowers, they have primary meanings of *love, luxury, nobility, refinement, a belle, rare beauty, Chinese symbol for many children, you flatter me,* and ***thoughtfulness***. My goodness! Orchids

Putting together an orchid garden such as this is simple and fun, and not much effort considering the impact it makes when it is presented as a gift.

have a lot to say, and that's not including the secondary meanings, which depending on the variety, will convey different messages entirely.

My tips on growing orchids are similar to those of many other plants—location is vitally important. And it is true that orchids are heavy feeders and require quite a bit of bright, indirect sunlight too. But the reality is, and this is my own opinion formed after many years of owning a flower shop full of orchids for sale, is that some plants, even from the same greenhouse, same stock line, same planting medium, same everything, simply resist blooming. It is up to the plant whether it likes to throw blooms or not. Sure, you can coax a few blooms out of non-blooming orchids periodically, and they'll look fine and healthy without blooms their entire lives. But you will either have a Betty Bloomer that is always full of year-round blossoms or a Debbie Downer that would rather die than bloom. Simple as that.

How to Create an Orchid Garden

MATERIALS

- Large display container—ceramic, wood, or a basket with a liner
- Orchids of your choice. I suggest three or more plants for an impactful display, but it is OK to use just one plant as well, depending on the size of your container. You can procure your orchids from whatever outlet you choose, be it a grocery store, local flower shop, or nursery. Repurpose or recycle the decorative pots they're sold in, leaving them in only their greenhouse pot liners.
- Drain rocks or pebbles
- Coconut coir or other sustainable filler
- Decorative top-dressing, such as beach glass, pebbles, or nature-found moss and twigs
- Support sticks such as branches you've foraged or natural bamboo sticks

INSTRUCTIONS

Add some drain pebbles to the bottom of the decorative container, filling enough so that when placed inside, the base of the orchid plant is up to the same level as the top of the decorative container.

Place your orchids strategically into the container, being mindful of the direction of the blooms on the stem, assuring they are facing forward and outward in a pleasing manner.

Once your orchids are in place, you need to fill the container all around the orchids to hold them in place. Do this by using sustainable products such as coconut coir, composted bark, or pine needles. We frequently want to use peat moss in these instances, and we have formed a bad habit in doing so. I myself am guilty of this bad habit, however I have not used peat for many years since learning about the jeopardized state of bogs and wetlands from where it's harvested. As stated earlier, peat moss is currently not a sustainable product, and it is not a good filler or dressing for plants either, as it harbors moisture, therefore creating a perfect environment for mildew and insects. Check the *Resource Directory* for sources of more sustainable alternatives to peat.

Once the container is filled with your chosen filler and the orchids feel secure in their place, top with decorations such as rock, glass pebbles, or forest-floor nature-led items.

Remove the painted support sticks and clips that normally come with commercially grown orchids and either repurpose or recycle them. Instead, use a more organic but elegant alternative such as natural bamboo sticks or gathered branches tied to the orchid stems with hemp twine, and then cover that with a beautiful silk ribbon.

ADDITIONAL LIVING HOUSEPLANTS

It's common to reach for non-living, and oftentimes impersonal things when it comes to procuring gifts for others, even when we are searching for a gift with real meaning. So, where can you go, and what can you buy that would convey very specific feelings and sentiments to another? There is no other gift that can do this, making a living plant that conveys messages in the language of flowers the idyllic accolade. In addition to the beautiful *Schefflera* pictured here, there is a plethora of houseplants that are rich with lovely messages and sentiments. All it takes is a little creativity in your presentations to make them into exemplary and meaningful presents for others. Here are five examples of houseplants that have useful sentiments in the language of flowers:

Also known as the Australian umbrella tree, the *Schefflera* conveys messages of **security, stability, enduring,** and **customary**. What a wonderful set of sentiments and a perfect gift for a housewarming, or for any occasion that pertains to the embarkment and initiation of new adventures or milestones.

- ❁ **Ficus** *Ficus microcarpa:* wisdom, understanding, unity, prosperity, and harmony
- ❁ **Peace lily** *Spathiphyllum:* compassion, optimism, and peace
- ❁ **Philodendron** *Philodendron bipinnatifidum:* prosperity, good health, and love of nature
- ❁ **Snake Plant** *Sansevieria*: aka mother-in-law's tongue: peace, tranquility, calmness, luck, positive energy, freshness, and balance
- ❁ **Spider plant** *Chlorophytum comosum:* stimulates chi energy, fertility, success, and abundance when hung in kitchen.

PART 2
Perpetual Posies & Sitting with Sentiments

What Is a Posy?

By modern definition, a posy is a petite bouquet of flowers, herbs, and plants that were intentionally chosen to convey a message in the language of flowers. In *The Posy Book*, I shared with you quite a lot about posies, including their long and intricate history, their various reinventions, and beautiful ways to make your own modernized posies. I also provided posy recipes and included detailed instructions on how to make these posies in a way that is cohesive with a contemporary floral arrangement. This book provides all these principles as well, with additional inspiration and instruction on how to create many more botanical gifts and styled floral arrangements besides posies. But it especially highlights the imperative and inspirational cohesiveness between creating a cutting garden—referred to as a *floriography garden* in this book—then using the flowers, herbs, and greens from these gardens to produce these intimate bouquets—posies—that tell a story. By creating a compilation of various greetings and sentiments using the language of flowers, a posy can serve as a vehicle to convey profound messages that cannot be articulated in words. They are chronicles of heartfelt messages and stories and are like a greeting card—but so much better because they are flowers! It is you who is gathering the various materials with their unique languages—therefore, posies are incredibly individualized for their recipient. I believe this is why they are so wholeheartedly appreciated and respected by the receiver, and the creator finds it very rewarding as well.

Imagine being able to walk through your cultivated floriography garden, big or small, or a lovely potted patio garden, and being able to cut your materials to construct a beautiful posy for a gift to a friend or loved one, or for yourself to enjoy indoors on the nightstand. It is possible to do this by planning, cultivating, and tending your purposeful plot so that you will always have flowers, foliage, herbs, plants, shrubs, and even branches readily available to create themed sentiments for posies. I love this type of purposeful garden planning and cultivating, and I am forever consciously curating my own garden for the purpose of creating these gifts from the garden. I find it hugely rewarding and I will never stop doing it. For me, the act of growing and cultivating beautiful blooms, cutting them, and creating lovely posies, bountiful bouquets, and other botanical treasures is a pleasure I will always hold dear to my heart. Creating gorgeous gifts from the garden is, in many ways, the same as preparing a nourishing meal for someone you care for, except these gifts provide nourishment psychologically, to both the giver and receiver, and they are also a glorious feast for the eyes. Do not be hesitant to cut from these gardens with worry that you will diminish or damage them. These are cutting gardens by design, and everything you grow in our garden will benefit from periodic pruning and shaping. Through the act of cutting from your garden to create beautiful things from your harvest, you are also tidying everything up, which prompts new growth and reflowering too.

Besides the illustrated floriography garden designs featured in this section, along with a list of the plant materials used in these illustrations and posies, there are also alternate and seasonal substitutions provided, which can be planted in addition to or in place of the featured plants in the gardens. It is OK if you cannot or do not wish to create these gardens in their entirety, as the idea is to plant a seed (pun intended), prompting you to cultivate a garden meant to provide specific sentiments.

Once you have selected and harvested your materials from the garden, or procured them elsewhere, you will learn how to arrange them into a posy or other floral gifts by utilizing the methods and tips provided in part 3, titled *"How to Arrange Posies and Bouquets."* You will learn techniques that will impart an aesthetic to your designs that will make you proud and worthy of a gift with a beautiful presentation.

SIMPLY *Sustainable*

From the beginning, whether you cultivate your garden from seeds, plugs, or plants, it is important to do it sustainably. There are many reasons why you should garden sustainably, and just as many—if not more—reasons to design with your materials sustainably. When we use the word sustainable in gardening, it translates into incorporating growing and care methods that uphold the plant's ability to survive and thrive with little input from us. That means the right plant in the right place, so that it can thrive without too much input from you. Small inputs, such as organic soil enhancements, pruning and maintaining the plant's health and structure, and providing the right environmental needs for the plant are sustainable gardening practices.

Sentiment Gardens
Providing Nature's Tonic

We are living in a task-based, screen-driven *hustle culture* where we're often in a race to the finish lines of productivity, wealth, worthiness, and sometimes even survival. This type of living can damp down our creative thinking and reduce our feelings of empathy for others. Even the simplest gestures of humanity might go undone or misunderstood. We can't always think straight because of the continuous bombardment of information that we don't know what to do with. We have become numbed to atrocities and wrongdoings, and collectively as a society we often tap out of our basic responsibilities as a human being requiring compassion, understanding, respect, and love. It's hard for us to celebrate, honor life's beautiful events and moments, and figure out any discourse that we may be experiencing when we cannot tune in to our inner creative thinking selves.

What if we created garden spaces that, through the symbolism and language of flowers, prompted us and allowed us to heal, to celebrate? To share love, sorrow, and friendship? These types of purposefully designed garden spaces are what I call "sentiment gardens." Sentiment gardens are designed as places to retreat to, to sit and rest, and to contemplate, all the while absorbing the symbolism and messages that come to you from the flowers, plants, and trees therein. Sentiment gardens command you to give pause and think, to reflect and then come to solutions. You might even leave with fresh ideas and feel inspired. The garden provides a space for us to open pathways to our hearts and minds and guides us inward to healing, rejuvenation, tranquility, and so much more.

A sentiment garden can be designed with your own choice of plants and their symbolism and messages, and even then, as you sit in the space, it is your choice which parts of these messages you take hold of. Sometimes you just need a little redirecting and other times, a deep reconstruction of your thoughts and feelings. And we all, from time to time, need answers to the complexities we face throughout our lives and a balm for our heartaches. Designing garden spaces with sentiments in mind can be a rewarding and rich experience to be enjoyed by you and anyone who visits this space for years and generations to come. They are an astonishing gift that keeps giving, year after year, providing rich and robust replenishment to its visitors.

In the following examples of sentiment gardens, you will see they are designed as rooms, or quadrants, courtyards, and even patio gardens. Some involve simple aesthetics or elaborate schemes, but all are themed by certain feelings or occasions. It is important to provide a place for comforting rest in these gardens—after all, the idea is to place yourself amid all the symbolism and sentiments and provide your physical body with the opportunity to take it all in.

Each sentiment garden follows a designated theme that is associated with the accompanying floriography garden and their posies. This proves the multitude of ways our gardens can be useful in conveying messages, thus providing the gifts they hold in both physiological and abstract ways.

I hope you will be inspired to create your own sentiment garden, allowing you to sit in quiet repose and immerse yourself—then invite others to join you in finding health and healing, comfort, joy, love, and celebration, and many more channels of enlightenment.

On Designing Gardens

When we think of a well-designed, beautiful garden, we must always think of colors and textures, as these are vital elements of good design, and they are usually the first thing we see and experience in our gardens. But a well-designed garden must also have bones and structure. By this, I mean hedges, trees, and other uniquely structured botanical elements. And there is a tree for every garden and every space—you just need to find the right one. There are beautiful trees that only reach a height of two feet and do not require large root areas, which means they will thrive in pots if given the right care. Architectural features such as an arbor on a patio or gracing a walkway, spheres and other garden art, stonework, and fountains provide more than just composition and focus; they can also serve to uphold vining or rambling plants or highlight

When I am among the trees,
especially the willows and the honey locust
equally the beech, the oaks and the pines,
they give off such hints of gladness.
I would almost say that they save me, and daily.
I am so distant from the hope of myself,
in which I have goodness, and discernment,
and never hurry through the world
but walk slowly, and bow often.
Around me the trees stir in their leaves
and call out, "Stay awhile."
The light flows from their branches.
And they call again, "It's simple," they say,
"and you too have come
into the world to do this, to go easy, to be filled
with light, and to shine."

— **Mary Oliver**

a unique and special tree or shrub. Structure and bones serve as year-round visual complements. Next, there should be a unified balance in the planting of perennials and annuals. Perennials are plants that grow back every year, and annuals, contrary to what their name implies, do not grow back every year. Both are your primary cutting materials, and I am constantly adding more of these into my garden. I tend use more perennials because there is a wider range of cutting materials available, but the annuals that are useful in posies and bouquets are also showstoppers in the garden. And although the annuals can be less varied, they are an integral part of good garden design and always provide structure and textural interest in the winter garden with their seed heads and skeletal remains of stems and foliage.

I encourage the use of native plants for the reason of sustainability, their benefits to local wildlife, and their ability to impart a naturalistic feel into your garden's design and the subsequent decor and gifts you create from their cuttings. Using native plants and foliage in floral design is a relatively new concept today, but historically, decorative wild and natural elements were usually the star of the show, where our hybridized plants and bred-to-perfection blooms tend to lead us away from nature and dominate our flower arrangements and other decorative items. The simplicity and diversity of native and wild elements can create elegant compositions both in and out of the garden.

Many of the plants and flowers listed throughout the book are natives of various regions of the United States, and I hope you will familiarize yourself with the native plants that are indigenous to your location and use them. Please refer to the *Resource Directory*, where you will find links to websites with lists of plants native to your locale.

The Gardens
& The Posies

Celebrations

There are so many things to celebrate in life! It is a bit of a challenge to compile just a few of the flowers and plants that convey celebratory messages because there are so many of them. And not only that, but even down to what sort of celebration you are engaging in and the plants that lend themselves perfectly to that kind of party or sentiment. Planting with the purpose of birthdays and other joyous celebrations is fun, and it is so convenient to have these festive messages available to gift on special days or times that need celebrating. Cutting just a few things featured here, or snipping from the entire garden, either way, a celebration posy is always a well-received gift.

For a detailed interpretation of the symbols (*, +, ++) used throughout this book, please refer to part 4, The New Language of Flowers Dictionary (Abridged), under "Essential Dictionary Notes."

THE CELEBRATIONS FLORIOGRAPHY GARDEN & LET'S CELEBRATE POSY

This *Celebrations Garden* reflects a mid-spring to early-summer seasonal compilation of flowers and foliage to create a multitude of joyous messages and symbolisms. Keep in mind that posies and other gifts don't always have to be *blooms*. As you see here, the Chinese fringe bush and chervil prove to be perfect messengers of *fun* and *gladness*, and they lend beautiful color and fun textures to the garden, its subsequent posies and other gifts.

THE *Celebrations* FLORIOGRAPHY GARDEN

- **Black currant**: elation, bliss
- **Chervil**: gladness, sincerity
- **Chinese fringe***: fun and flirty
- **Crown vetch (aka purple crown vetch)**: success to you, success crowned you
- **Daffodil+, several stems**: celebrate, joy++
- **Hazel tree**: divination, poetic inspiration, creative inspiration, wishes, reconciliation++
- **Hyacinth**, pink color: playful joy, play
- **Jasmine**: transport of joy, cheerfulness, folly, glee++
- *Pieris*: happy thoughts
- **Guelder rose (*Viburnum opulus*, aka snowball tree, cramp bark, European cranberry-bush)**: good news, goodness++
- **Quince (*Chaenomeles japonica*, flowering, aka Japanese quince)**: cheers my soul, abundance++

ALTERNATE AND SEASONAL *Variations*

- *Artemisia* (*Artemisia vulgaris*, aka mugwort): happiness, good luck++
- *Anthurium* (aka little boy flower, flamingo flower): happiness, abundance++
- *Chrysanthemum*+: cheerfulness, long life, optimism++
- *Cotoneaster*: artful, fun in abundance
- *Gaura** (*Oenothera L.*, aka Siskiyou pink, wand flower, bee blossom): exhilarating, lively++
- *Geum**: cheerful, delightful, future is waiting with open arms, works as a prayer++
- **Indian Heliotrope** (*Heliotropium indicum*, aka indian turnsole): intoxicated with joy++
- **Liatris** (aka gayfeather): gaiety, bliss, joy++
- **Parsley**: festivity, gratitude, thanks, useful knowledge, a feast, lasting pleasures.
- **Sun cups** (*Oenothera fruticosa* L., aka sundrops, narrowleaf evening primrose): happiness, happy love++

How many times have you said, *What can I get them for their birthday? They already have everything they need!* Imagine having something meaningful, purposeful, beautiful, and well-received at your fingertips at all times. For many years, I have both professionally and personally gifted posies for all sorts of celebrations. I can say without hesitation that it is truly an impactful gift that will not soon be forgotten. A lunch or dinner out with a movie will last for a day, but a posy will last for a week or more, and the sentiment tag will serve as a memento for years to come. I have created some gorgeous sentiment tags for celebration posies, and they really do become cherished keepsakes for the recipient, and they make wonderful bookmarks too!

CELEBRATIONS GARDENS AND POSIES

THE CELEBRATORY SENTIMENT GARDEN

A sentiment garden for sitting and reflecting on life's bountiful wins, accomplishments, milestones, and achievements is a remarkable way to let the good feelings seep in and stay a while. Once you're in this space, you can really relish all the upsides of life. It's not often we get to do that, to just sit and think about all the good things that happen in life, right? And it's so important to do this, and that's what this sweet and beautiful spot will do for you. This garden represents the summer season, and is a sample of just a few of the many different plants and flowers that convey joyous and congratulatory sentiments—so go ahead and have fun with this!

THE *Celebratory* SENTIMENT GARDEN

- **Bay laurel (*Lauris nobilis*, aka sweet bay, bay tree, Grecian laurel):** personal achievement, success, reward of merit, nobility, praise++
- **Cosmos (*Cosmos bipinnatus+*, white color):** joy in love and life
- ***Hardenbergia**** (aka coral pea, happy wanderer, vine lilac):** spirited, happiness, capability, ingenuity
- **Ixia (aka wand flower, African corn lily):** happiness
- **Lemon balm (*Melissa officinalis*):** healing, fun, brings love, jokes, pleasantry++
- **Lily (yellow color):** I'm walking on air!
- **Roses (red and yellow together):** happiness, celebration, joy, excitement, gaiety, congratulations
- **Sweet marjoram (aka oregano):** joy, happiness, kindness, birth++

Garden Notes

- **Lilies**, either Asiatic or Oriental, work so perfectly planted in pots. This is an easy way to add drama and color to anywhere in the garden, and the nice thing about it is that you can just leave them in the pots and layer other plants such as perennials atop them for color and interest during the bulbs' off-season. Additionally, you don't have to worry about gophers or moles eating them as you would if planted underground, however, an occasional squirrel may present an issue by digging them out of the pots. To prevent this, place a grid of chicken wire over the top of the soil just above the bulbs so they cannot access them should a creature try to dig them up. If you are layering perennials on top, just add more soil and plant them right over the chicken wire.

- **White cosmos** (or any type or color cosmos!) are an absolute joy and delight to grow. Regular deadheading keeps the blooms coming all summer into fall, and if you stop deadheading in late summer and let a few heads go to seeds, you can use those seeds the next year as they are very simple to germinate and grow. These are such whimsical and beautiful flowers that provide lots of pollen and nectar in the garden, and they are absolutely dreamy in posies and bouquets too!

- **Lemon balm**, for as much as we love it, requires a word of caution. If you plant directly in the garden and are in a climate that is somewhat mild, you will be catching and pulling runners up to keep it from taking over the garden for a very, very long time! Best to plant in a large pot to prevent this. Still, all the good things about lemon balm far outweigh the bad, as it's a very useful herb in teas, bouquets, and posies.

TERMS OF ENDEARMENT

There is no emotion so powerful as love, and we all carry this emotion in various forms and levels in our hearts, souls, and minds. If there is any emotion that floriography is exceptionally good at expressing, it is love. Whether you would like to show your lover you cannot live without them, or you would like to convey sweet sentiments of parental or familial love to your children, aunt, or any other family member, this garden will accommodate an abundance of ways to express the many natures of love.

THE TERMS OF ENDEARMENT FLORIOGRAPHY GARDEN & ALL ABOUT LOVE POSY

This garden design represents a summer compilation of plants that provide an abundance of love-centered messages to choose from. It is possible to use all elements from this garden, as shown in the subsequent posy, or just use a few essentials, or even one type of flower in the form of a gorgeous en mass, monobotanical bouquet from it. There is enormous versatility for expressing love in the language of flowers!

THE *Terms of Endearment* FLORIOGRAPHY GARDEN

- *Agonis** (aka burgundy willow, peppermint willow, willow myrtle): attraction, balance, grace, poise, versatility
- **Angel vine***: delightful entrapment, steadiness, infinite affections, creativity, protection
- *Celosia* (aka feather amaranth, princess feather): symbol of affection++
- **Chocolate cosmos** (*Cosmos bipinnatus**): simple pleasures, the deepest love for you
- **Globe amaranth** (*Gomphrena globosa*): unfading love, constant, unchangeable or immortal love
- *Hydrangea:* happiness, haven, devotion, remembrance++
- *Pittosporum** (aka cheesewood): blessings, shelter, comfort++
- **Rose, pink color:** beauty++
- **Rose, red color**: love, beauty, charm, desire, passion++
- *Scabiosa* (aka pincushion flower): admiration++
- **Sweet William** (*Dianthus barbatus,* aka pinks): grant me one smile, affection, love++

ALTERNATE AND SEASONAL *Variations*

- **Almond tree:** abiding love and friendship, hope, wisdom++
- **Carnation, hot pink color:** ardent love
- **Forget-me-not:** hope, remembrance, true love, faithful love
- **Heliotrope (*Heliotropium arborescens*, aka cherry pie, garden heliotrope):** devotion, I adore you, herb of love, eternal love, I love you, intoxicated with pleasure++
- ***Hibiscus syriacus* (common garden, aka rose of Sharon):** consumed by love, persuasion
- **Lemon verbena:** attracts love and fidelity, attracts the opposite sex
- **Lilac+ *(Syringa)*:** love, beauty, earliest first love, do you still love me?++
- **Madrone (*Arbutus menziesii* aka Pacific madrone):** thee only do I love, you are my only love, esteem and love
- **Scarlet fuchsia (*Graptophyllum excelsum*):** will you confide in love, delicate charms, the ambition in my love thus plagues itself
- ***Stephanotis* (aka Madagascar jasmine):** wedding, marital happiness, desire to travel

There are countless times in our lives when we want someone to know how much we love them, and it does not always need to be, nor should be, only to commemorate occasions such as Valentine's Day, an anniversary, or a wedding. But these occasions certainly denote showering and showing your love with flowers! Love abounds at all types and intensities, and it does our hearts good to simply say "I love you" for no reason at all other than to say it.

THE LOVE AND ADORATION SENTIMENT GARDEN

The love and adoration sentiment garden depicts the late summer and autumn season. With boundless opportunities to pick and choose your own plants to create loving sentiments and messages, you could add a few elements to this garden that would bring forth spring and summer blooms and beautiful foliage as well. Beautiful pots full of spring bulbs and planters of summer bulbs layered atop with summer perennials would be a lovely addition and would carry this garden through all seasons with the sentiments of love.

THE *Love & Adoration* SENTIMENT GARDEN

- **Apple**: love, prosperity, abundance, strength, beauty, art, and poetry++
- **Belladonna lily (aka *Amaryllis belladonna*, naked ladies, Jersey lily, March lily)**: pure loveliness, I dream of you, you are a dream, beautiful but timid or silent
- *Chrysanthemum*+: cheerfulness, love, optimism++
- *Dahlia*, **yellow color**: I am happy that you love me
- *Pelargonium* **(geraniums+)**: conjugal affection++
- **Stock (aka wallflower, clove flower, gilly flower)**: bonds of affection, happy life, contented life, lasting beauty++

Garden Notes

- When cultivating and caring for hedging plants such as *Pittosporum* and *Agonis*, it is a good idea to prune regularly. This not only keeps the plant tidy and accessible for cutting but also keeps new growth coming, thus preventing it from becoming too woody.

- Roses are heavy feeders! Fertilize regularly with an organic fertilizer with an NPK ratio of 3-5-3. The middle number represents phosphorus, which is what the rose needs for blooms and roots. Read your fertilizer instructions, but generally, you'll want to use half a cup to one cup per rose plant.

- Chocolate cosmos are tender perennials and winter hardy only in USDA zones 9–11, but they are grown from *Dahlia*-like tubers, so in colder climates, you should dig them up and bring them indoors for the winter. They are incredibly worth it! They will put on a show in the garden all summer long, and I don't believe I use any flower more in posies during the spring, summer, and fall than this one, as it means ***simple pleasures*** and ***the deepest love for you.*** Such versatile sentiments, and they really do smell just like chocolate!

HEALTH AND HEALING

Inevitably, there are times when we need to impart healing and healthful wishes to one another, and to our own selves as well. This garden, and the posies and other gifts that you can give and receive from its abundance, offer bright, beautiful, and uplifting messages to anyone that may be feeling poorly, recovering from physical adversities, fighting ongoing illness, or just need a lift with healing energies. Did you know that happiness strengthens your arteries? Yes, it sure does! And a beautiful health and healing garden with its many gifts and therapeutic messages are sure to bring a smile, making it beneficial in moving one toward comfort and well-being.

THE HEALTH AND HEALING FLORIOGRAPHY GARDEN & HEALING WISHES POSY

When all the ingredients from this garden are used to create a posy such as a *Healing Wishes Posy,* the result is a gorgeous floral arrangement that emits joy, happiness, and wellness. Reflecting a summer garden, the color palette is purposely bright and uplifting, assuring a favorable reaction when one is subjected to a happy compilation such as this. Also, one could pinch the chamomile blossoms out of the posy to brew a cup of hot chamomile tea. Isn't that lovely?

There are many parallels between the meanings of certain flowers and plants and their medicinal and culinary uses and values. In the following "Garden Notes" section, I have highlighted some of the plants featured in this garden as well as the following sentiment garden along with their medicinal attributes.

THE *Health and Healing* FLORIOGRAPHY GARDEN

- *Calendula* **(aka pot marigold)**: health, cares, joy, constancy, remembrance++

- **Chamomile, garden (*Anthemis nobilis*):** energy in action, healing, comfort, fortitude, love in adversity++

- **Cornflower (*Centaurea cyanus*, aka bachelor's button):** healing properties, hope, patience, love++

- **Dill:** soothing

- **Elderberry (*Sambucus*):** compassion, kindness

- **Pine:** endurance, light, longevity++

- **Solidaster (*Solidago*, aka goldenrod):** encouragement++

- **Roses, yellow and white together:** harmony

ALTERNATE AND SEASONAL *Variations*

- **Apple:** healing, transformation++
- **Cottonwood tree (aka balm of Gilead):** relief, cure
- ***Sempervivum*** **(aka hens and chicks, echeveria, houseleek):** long life, vivacity, robust, resilience, domestic economy++
- ***Echinacea*** **(aka purple cone flower):** capability, skill, strength, health, shield++
- **Garlic chives:** courage, protection, strength
- **Ginger:** pleasant, safe, warming, comforting++
- **Golden rain tree (*Cassia fistula*, aka golden shower tree):** ray of sunshine, promise, health, healing, radiance
- **Lavender:** healing, calming, soothing the passions of the heart, faithful, constancy++
- **Mānuka (*Leptospermum scoparium*, aka New Zealand tea tree, tea tree):** healing, strong health++
- **Willow:** serenity, strongly healing++

The beauty of the flowers in a posy is always a delight, but when the recipient decodes all the messages of well-being and care, it elevates the compilation to an incredibly touching gift. It is a perfect gathering of restorative colors and inviting textures, and these two things alone generate a healing effect. It's been proven many times over that flowers make people happy, and happiness promotes health. So, this posy is just what the doctor ordered!

HEALTH AND HEALING GARDENS AND POSIES

THE HEALING AND RESTORATION SENTIMENT GARDEN

It is well documented and proven that being in places of nature promotes wellness in our mental and physical health. The line that separates us as humans from nature is porous, and with practice we can subvert that line and thus setting us into a space where our thinking process is less directed and restricted. Creating a space that encompasses sentiments of healing and restoration will provide your mind and body with the opportunity to recharge, both inside and out. And it's not difficult to create a space for this vital act. You do not need large, expansive areas or formal gardens. Rather, simple and comfortable seating surrounded by some selective flowers and plants will suffice. The trick is that you've got to think about the plants that are around you, and you have to be receptive and contemplate all their wondrous messages to you.

THE *Healing* & *Restoration* SENTIMENT GARDEN

- **Black poplar**: courage++
- **Feverfew (*Tanacetum parthenium L.*)**: good health, warmth, you light up my life, protection
- **Heather, white color**: tranquility, protection from danger
- **Hyssop (*Hyssopus officinalis*)**: cleansing, purification, holy herb that wards off evil and evil spirits, calmness, holiness
- **Flowering moss (*Pyxidanthera barbulata*, aka pixie moss)**: life is sweet
- **Lemon tree:** healing, love trees, zeal++
- **Mullein (*Verbascum thapsus*, aka great mullein, greater mullein, common mullein)**: good nature, take courage, health
- **Oak tree:** healing, protection, strength, endurance++
- **Petunia:** your presence soothes me++

THE MENTAL AND PHYSICAL GIFTS WE RECEIVE

As early as 1796, nature-led, horticulture-based treatment for persons with mental illness was prominent in Europe and consisted of active flower and vegetable gardening as well as garden settings for rest and recreation. In subsequent years, the United States began using gardening and nature to successfully treat mental illness as well. It was not until the 1950s that the treatment of mental illness shifted radically due to the introduction of new and powerful drugs. This resulted in drug therapy taking the lead in treatment for all sorts of psychosis. Unfortunately, along with the introduction of drug therapy, treatment centers with natural settings that facilitate horticulture activities began to disappear. We slowly removed gardens, greenhouses, and parklike places that provided serenity and the restful appreciation of nature for clients that suffered from mental illness. And while we certainly appreciate and admire advancements in the treatments afforded by modern medicine, it is disheartening and sad that these nature-centered treatment methods have been mostly replaced with drugs and unnatural living environments with little access to fresh air, let alone a garden to sit in or a plant to take care of. It is a shame, while we know that nature has a proven track record of ushering and facilitating mental health and wellness, that we would overlook this method in modern treatments. I believe wholeheartedly that it should be embraced and implemented as often as possible in treatments.

Thankfully, today we are slowly coming full circle and are traveling in the right direction. Horticultural therapy is a *thing*, and it's alive and well in all its modalities, and is again being credited and practiced as a highly effective tool to treat the mind and body. This wonderful, collaborative step in the right direction engages natural wellness, therapy gardens, and horticulture activities for use at a multitude of programs both inside and outside hospital environments around the world. It is refreshing, and a relief to know that both horticulture specialists and medical professionals are believing in the power of nature, and they can attest to the success in treatment of both mental and physical ailments with nature's multiple gifts.

Even still, when we have physical ailments and distress in our bodies, we tend to reach toward the medicine cabinet instead of looking to nature and our gardens. By cultivating and taking rest in our health and healing gardens, we can tap into nature's powerful boost and connect our minds to the healing properties that are around us. Our bodies are designed to repair themselves, and making this connection provides that avenue for this to happen.

> *"I cannot say exactly how nature exerts its calming and organizing effects on our brains, but I have seen in my patients the restorative and healing powers of nature and gardens, even for those who are deeply disabled neurologically. In many cases, gardens and nature are more powerful than any medication."*
>
> —Oliver Sacks

It will take practice for most of us, but by learning to sit quietly and absorb all the symbolism and messages of health and healing around us, we will become more able to withstand the adversities of ill health and heal from within.

You can learn more about horticultural therapy by visiting the website of the American Horticultural Therapy Association at ahta.memberclicks.net.

Garden Notes

- Pine can be grown in many forms and variants of the genus. It does not always have to be a large tree! I love the dwarf varieties scattered in the garden . . . around rocks, hillsides, and even in large urns or planters.

- Flowering moss, or pixie moss, is not moss at all but a member of the Diapensiaceae family of plants, which are native to the Eastern United States. Their natural habitat is dry, sandy soil, and usually under pines. They will tolerate full sun, but they do not like to share their space with much of anything else. If you can find the right spot for them, they are an absolute delight in the garden. They lend magic, mystery, and sweetness to the environment, hence its meaning, *life is sweet.*

- I have included a few of the many herbs and plants that are used in herbal medicine in the posy and gardens. This does not mean that I advise you to use them as medicine, as I am not a physician or herbalist. (see the "How to Use This Book," on page XVI, for my disclaimer on this!) Here are some of the herbs featured, and their traditional medicinal attributes in the form of teas:

  - **Chamomile**: menstrual cramps, diabetes and blood sugar, inflammation, osteoporosis, cancer, sleep and relaxation, cold symptoms, and mild skin conditions

  - **Hyssop** (*Hyssopus officinalis*): cold and flu, coughs, sore throat, digestion, sedative, weight loss, antimicrobial, muscle pain, heart and circulatory, and hormones

  - **Spearmint**: digestive, antioxidant, hormone imbalance, memory, bacterial infections, blood sugar, stress, arthritis, and blood pressure

GRATITUDE AND THANKS

When my daughters were young, our family would often begin our meals together by each of us sharing one thing that happened to or for them or that they observed that day for which they were grateful. I know they carry this small but meaningful ritual with them still today, and I know that they will guide their own children to this practice too. I love starting a meal with a prayer and an acknowledgment to at least one of a host of things I am grateful for. Saying ***thank you*** and expressing gratitude has enormously positive effects on our minds and bodies. Expressing gratitude disconnects us from any negative emotions and sends a revitalizing charge throughout our minds and bodies. Flowers go hand in hand with happiness, and they are an expert relater of gratitude and thanks. Having a cutting garden with grateful sentiments provides you with copious ways to recognize gratitude and being thankful for anything. Of all the floriography gardens you could devise, this one would be the most useful, because saying thank you and showing gratitude should never be spared, and in fact extensively used one way or another.

THE GRATITUDE AND THANKS FLORIOGRAPHY GARDEN & THANK-YOU POSY

Container gardening is underrated, and here is proof. You truly *can* grow virtually anything you desire inside pots as long as you meet the plant's requirements to thrive, which are, in most cases, attainable to you. The *Gratitude and Thanks Garden* is a compilation of summer and fall blooms, except for a rare and unusual bloom in the late summer from a forsythia. Typically, *Forsythia* is a blooming hallmark of spring, but I have one that will occasionally throw a small round of blooms in the fall. This happens when the plant experiences extreme conditions such as heat and drought, which occur frequently in California, and then when fall weather arrives and settles the conditions, the plant is tricked into thinking it is spring. When it happens, I think, *Since the blooms are there, why not use them?* Remember, you can also use the foliage of the plant when blooms are not available, and vice versa, and it will mean the same thing unless it is otherwise specified in the dictionary.

THE *Gratitude* & *Thanks* FLORIOGRAPHY GARDEN

- *Alstroemeria* (aka Peruvian lily, Inca lily): friendship, devotion, aspiring, wealth, prosperity, fortune
- *Begonia:* cordiality, long beautiful, goodness++
- *Dahlia+*: gratitude, dignity, eloquence++
- *Forsythia:* good nature, anticipation
- **Mint:** warmth of feeling++
- **Rose, peach color:** appreciation
- **Sage:** gratitude, esteem++
- **Sweet marjoram (aka oregano):** kindness, courtesy++
- **Geranium, silver-leaf** (*Pelargonium sidoides*): admiration, recall

ALTERNATE AND SEASONAL *Variations*

- *Abelia:* gratitude
- *Azalea* (*Rhododendron spp.*): gratitude, temperance, take care++
- *Campanula* (aka canterbury bells): gratitude, thinking of you++
- **Cotton:** well-being, gratitude, obligations++
- *Delphinium:* well-being, sweetness, lightness, levity, lightness, bighearted++
- *Gladiolus:* generosity, strength of character, I'm sincere++
- **Globe flower** (aka *Trollius*): generosity, gratitude
- **Loosestrife** (*Lysimachia*): wishes granted
- **Rose, deep pink color:** thankfulness, gratitude
- **Sage, purple-leaf:** gratitude

If someone has touched your life in some way, then a beautiful posy designed to convey the sentiments of gratitude would be such an impactful and memorable way to show them. And there are times that a greeting card may do to say thank you, but imagine receiving this posy instead, where the blossoms do the talking and leave the recipient with an overwhelming sense of happiness and well-being. And just imagine, everything in this beautiful posy was grown in pots!

GRATITUDE AND THANKS GARDENS AND POSIES

THE GRATEFUL REFLECTIONS SENTIMENT GARDEN

If you experience something amazing, why don't you sit *in* it and sit *with* it. Let yourself feel grateful and claim the beauty of your world. There is no better balm for the soul than to rest and relish in the good! That is what a grateful sentiment garden does, enabling us to fully savor all things big and small for which we are grateful. This gorgeous garden represents the spring season and contains a few of my favorite blooms and trees. Notice there are not a whole lot of different plants and flowers. There are just six in this illustration, which provides enough powerful messages and sentiments to make relaxing here a joyous and enlightening experience.

THE *Grateful Reflections* SENTIMENT GARDEN

- *Camellia+*: contentment, beauty, excellence, loveliness, gratitude++
- *Campanula*, **white color (aka bellflower)**: gratitude
- **Columbine+** (*Aquilegia*, **yellow color**): lightness, happiness
- **Crocus+**: cheerfulness, joy, pleasure of hope, youthful gladness++
- *Pittosporum** **(aka cheesewood)**: blessings, to bring certainty, blessing++
- **Snowbell, Japanese** (*Styrax japonicus*): good fortune, blessing++

Garden Notes

- Japanese snowbell trees are a bit finicky to grow, so you need to find the right spot for them. They are acid-loving trees and prefer rich and well-draining soil. Depending on your soil's mineral makeup, you may consider adding an acid-producing amendment such as sulfur or iron sulfate to your planting hole. They will not tolerate a lot of wind, so they will need some shelter from that to keep them happy, and they have a horizontal growth form—so make sure to place them where their broad canopy of growth can be accommodated. All this fuss is worth it though, because the bell-shaped clusters of blooms are one of the sweetest things in a garden, not to mention a cotton-candy fragrance. And who doesn't need a little **good fortune** and **blessings** brought to them from their garden?
- *Camellias* prefer partial shade and diffused lighting but will tolerate a few hours of direct morning sunlight. They should be planted or, if potted, placed in an area that does not receive the harsh, direct rays of the afternoon sun as this will cause the foliage to scorch. Do not fertilize your *Camellias*—commercial fertilizers tend to be too strong. If you think they need a boost, you can sprinkle some bone or blood meal around the base in early spring or early fall.

PRAYER AND MEDITATION

Using the garden and flowers as a sanctuary and catalyst for meditation and prayer is not a new concept or discipline. The garden has been a place for prayer since biblical times, with reference to the Garden of Gethsemane in which Jesus goes to pray during his weakest, most vulnerable, and treacherous episodes in his life. And although using the garden and its flowers for a place of peace, quiet, and reflection has been in practice for millennia, the term *meditate* and it's place in our gardens, both public and private, is somewhat modernistic. Nowadays, we have finally conceded that the use of flowers and gardens, and practicing meditation inside the garden, has profound effects on our mindfulness and overall well-being.

THE FAITH AND RESILIENCE FLORIOGRAPHY GARDEN & FAITH AND RESILIENCE POSY

How often do we need to send our thoughts and messages to dear friends and loved ones who need a boost in resilience? It frequently goes undone, but so many of us lose our footing amid discourses and we lose sight of why things happen the way they do. We need fortitude, faith, and resilience, and a posy and other gifts that you can give and receive from a garden such as this can offer hope, peace, encouragement, and much more.

THE *Faith & Resilience* FLORIOGRAPHY GARDEN

- *Abutilon* (aka flowering maple): meditation, grace, dignity, enlightenment
- *Anemone:* faith
- *Astrantia;* (aka masterwort): strength, power, courage, protection
- *Hazel:* peace, divination, epiphanies, reconciliation++
- *Hydrangea:* devotion, haven, gracefulness, heartfelt praise, protection++
- *Passion flower* (*Passiflora caerulea*): Christian faith, belief, holy love, unpretentious++
- *Pelargonium*, geraniums: general; peaceful mind++
- *Queen Anne's Lace* (*Ammi majus*, aka bishop's flower): haven, sanctuary, protection, warmth++
- *Thyme* (*Thymus vulgaris*): affection, bravery, courage++

ALTERNATE AND SEASONAL *Variations*

- **Bird of paradise:** a symbol of faithfulness, magnificence, splendor++
- **California pepper tree (*Schinus*):** religious enthusiasm, sweetness, beauty, wit
- **Columbine + (*Aquilegia*):** gifts of the holy spirit, wisdom, salvation ++
- **Flowering cherry:** spiritual beauty, celebration of new beginnings
- ***Gentiana*, fringed:** I look to heaven, loveliness
- **Heliotrope (*Heliotropium arborescens*, aka cherry pie, garden heliotrope):** Godly devotion, forgiveness, acceptance, I remain true++
- **Lotus (*Nymphaea lotus*):** purity, elegance, holy spiritual flower, silence, beauty, elegance, spiritual promises++
- **Sandalwood:** spiritual empowerment, calmness in meditation, deep meditation
- **Silver Fir (*Abies alba, Abies amabilis*):** what you seek shall be found++
- **Vetiver (*Chrysopogon zizanioides*, aka khus):** tranquility, grounding, harmony

I cannot think of anything else in the world that would make someone feel like they've been given such a lift in their spirit and a boost in their mindset than this posy . . . other than a nice, long warm hug given along with it. There are too many times to count when I have needed this posy myself and wonder why I haven't made myself one to take in all this goodness in the sentiments and beauty for some get-up-and-go. And what a joy to create this posy for someone else! As I always say, you reap what you sow, and here is an example of a lot of goodness coming back your way!

THE PRAYER AND MEDITATION SENTIMENT GARDEN

Cultivating a garden that cues us to quietness and leads us to inner peace and spiritual awareness can work wonders on our mental and physical well-being. For this reason, these gardens, and the practice of sitting within them should be integrated into our daily lives as much as possible. I like to call this *horticultural intervention,* because it can work like a pill prescription, except it is so much better for us. The garden and nature are so good at organizing and calming our brains, and I find that when I am off-centered and without clear and concise direction and focus, a serene garden space reminds me of nature's abundant samples of order and renewal, miracles, beauty, and the soft-spoken symbolism and messages that are conveyed to me. Because of our concentration on the messages and symbolic meanings of the plants in the sentiment garden, we have directed and funneled our thoughts and energies toward a desired result, which in most cases results in settled and welcomed feelings about a particular subject or condition.

This serene *Prayer and Meditation* sentiment garden reflects the summer season and enhances our ability to reach our meditative state a little easier with its soft palette and tender textures. It is very inviting, and with practice, a garden like this can elevate us in many wonderful and favorable ways.

THE *Prayer & Meditation* SENTIMENT GARDEN

- **Blueberry:** healing, prayer, protection++
- *Penstemon* **(aka beard-tongue):** spiritual knowledge, understanding
- *Plumbago:* holy wishes, spiritual desire++
- **Stonecrop** (*Sedum villosum*)**:** tranquility, welcome
- **Sweet woodruff** (*Galium*)**:** patience, humility
- **Willow:** serenity, freedom++

Garden Notes

- The Geraniaceae family, including the genus *Pelargonium* and all their varieties, are stalwarts of floriography gardens, posies, and all other gifts of floriography. In every way they are just perfect! Their broad and general meanings in the language of flowers encapsulate so much of what we want to say for most occasions, and their aesthetic in floral design add textures, fragrance, and unique shapes and colors. All of these attributes serve them well planted in the garden as well as planted in pots, too, in fact, they are a classic plant for terra-cotta pots. They are one of the easiest potted plants that you can grow, often seemingly thriving on neglect (although I'm not saying to neglect them!). Few, if any garden pests bother these plants, and they will tolerate temps down to approximately 20–25°F.

- Let's all grow blueberries! There are so many varieties available to us, and at least one or more will be suitable for your gardening zone. They can be grown in pots, too, and they make such whimsical and fun additions to your potted gardens. Besides, they are delicious and so nutritious, especially when you have grown them yourself!

>
> *In our quest for perfection, we tend to deviate from nature, as a culture, and often find ourselves on some slippery slopes. A meditation and prayer garden can help us to circle back to nature. When we sit in these spaces that we have specifically designed to convey peace and meditative messages, solitude is allowed to seep in.*

Bereavement and Loss

When we lose a loved one, whether it is a person or a pet, although we do appreciate others' kind words to us, there is nothing that people can do to take the pain of loss away. Bereavement is the state of grief when the emotions are most profound and deeply felt, and sometimes the mere idea of living without a loved one is just too much. This is a time when words and messages from friends, colleagues, and loved ones can seem mere and modest. So, how do you convey and communicate your sorrow and regards to them, and at the same time, recognize *their* sorrow and your intense sadness and feelings *for them* during their time of loss and grief? Only flowers and their uplifting and heartfelt sentiments can do that. The language of flowers and their messages and sentiments transcend anything remotely possible with words. A gift of flowers, with their decoded messages on beautiful keepsake sentiment tags and cards, will mean the world to them, and not just for a short while. A gift like this is long remembered, and the sentiment tag attached to your gift will be a treasured token of your thoughtfulness for years to come.

THE BEREAVEMENT AND LOSS FLORIOGRAPHY GARDEN & BEREAVEMENT POSY

I am impressed with and truly appreciate how flowers and their meanings are so interchangeable and accommodating in our gardens and gifting. Their adaptability is evident in this *Bereavement and Loss Floriography Garden*, where most of these flowers can be interchanged to accommodate posies for numerous other occasions and sentiments in addition to, and as portrayed here in the sorrow and loss sentiments. *Hydrangea* can also impart sentiments of **pride**, **remembrance**, and **understanding**, and heliotrope works so lovely in a posy or bouquet to express **love** and **devotion**. The lamb's ear is perfect for someone who just needs **protection** and **support**, the *Scabiosa* is appropriate for loss, but also **admiration**, and the attar of roses, with its meaning of **gentility** and **preference** could work for almost any posy or other floral gift.

THE *Bereavement & Loss* FLORIOGRAPHY GARDEN

- **Chrysanthemum, white color:** loyal love, hope, truth
- **Geranium (*Pelargonium graveolens*):** aka rose-scented, attar of roses; preference, gentility, spiritual happiness++
- **Heliotrope (*Heliotropium arborescens*, aka cherry pie, garden heliotrope):** I adore you, eternal love ++
- *Hydrangea:* devotion, remembrance ++
- **Lamb's ear:** softness, support, spiritual borders
- *Scabiosa:* aka pincushion; comfort in the loss of someone, one that is dear++
- **Rose, white color:** eternal love, flower of light
- **Rosemary:** remembrance, constancy ++
- **Yarrow (*Achillea millefolium*):** cure for heartache, heals wounds, health, sorrow (in times of war) to dispel melancholy and heartache++

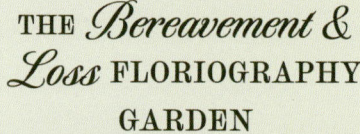

ALTERNATE AND SEASONAL *Variations*

- *Asclepias* (aka butterfly weed, milkweed, swallow-wort): hope in misery, medicine, cure for heartache, let me go
- Aster (*Tradescanti*, aka Michaelmas daisy, New England aster, Belgian aster, New York Aster): memories, farewell, healthy emotions, loyal love++
- *Brugmansia* (aka angel's trumpets): kind thoughts of those dearly departed, separation++
- Dill: soothing
- Everlasting (*Helichrysum italicum*, aka immortelle): never-ceasing memory, perpetual remembrance, endless love
- Flowering reed: confidence in heaven
- Hyacinth, purple color: sorrow
- Mugwort (*Artemisa vulgaris*): tranquility, dignity++
- Quince, flowering (*Chaenomeles japonica*, aka Japanese quince): cheers my soul, excellence
- Snowberry: heavenly thoughts

a posy for you
The Bereavement Posy

White Rose; eternal love, flower of light
Attar of Rose; preference, gentility
White Chrysanthemum; loyal love
Yarrow; cure for heartache
Heliotrope; I adore you, eternal love
Rosemary; remembrance
Scabiosa; one that is dear
Lamb's Ear; softness, support
Hydrangea; devotion, remembrance

I will never forget how I felt when I received a posy from my daughter after the shocking and untimely passing of my mother. When I first laid eyes on this posy and its sentiments, my heart nearly exploded with emotion. First, my mother would have loved it. And second, I thought of how lovely it was that we were honoring her with this beautiful creation of flowers and herbs, all put together with such thought and consideration. Each flower used in the posy conveyed healing messages, and when I read the sentiment tag line by line, I recall thinking, *Yes, I do feel this, and yes, this will happen with time.* This gorgeous and loving gift prompted my healing to begin, and although the pain in my heart was so raw and real, the pure sweetness of this gesture lightened it. It made me feel I was not alone in my deep sorrow and sadness and that my family knew I was experiencing these painful and deep emotions. This is what enabled me to begin my mourning process in a beneficial way.

THE SORROW AND GRIEF SENTIMENT GARDEN

The course of a garden, through its seasons and cycles, helps us to recognize and accept our grieving hearts with time. The grief itself is in knowing that time is passing without your loved ones and can be extremely difficult, but at the same time, if we acknowledge this passing of time, and our stories continue without a loved one, there can be healing.

Sitting and contemplating in a grief garden can be an incredibly healing experience. It should be made into habit when grief and sorrow are present, and just like anything that does us good, it can be a challenge to fit into our daily or weekly rituals.

This sentiment garden is situated in the spring and summer season and reflects a diverse planting of some of the most significant symbolisms of sorrow and grief. Some sentiments are uplifting and promising, and some demand attention to your sadness. Both are necessary to impart the grieving process and healing. I love sitting in a sentiment garden such as this and thinking of my mother not only because she loved roses and aloes (I am quite sure she loved all flowers and plants!) but also because the garden can help us hold on to memories too. And when we have a memory of loved ones, then they are still with us in a way, which is especially healing because it places us in a time and place with them.

THE *Sorrow & Grief* SENTIMENT GARDEN

- *Aloe vera:* overcomes grief, most effective healer++
- **Lady's mantle** (*Alchemilla mollis*, aka dew cups): comforting love, soft
- **Lovage:** strength, bring love
- **Pansy, wild** (aka viola tricolor, heart's ease, Johnny-jump-up): loving thoughts, reflection, happy thoughts
- **Spruce:** farewell, eternal hardiness, endurance
- **Tea rose:** I will always remember you
- *Zinnia*, **yellow color:** daily remembrance

Garden Notes

- *Zinnia* means "thoughts of absent friends," and "I miss you," which is a lovely thing to contemplate in a garden or posy. But the yellow-color *Zinnia* specifically means **daily remembrance**. It is wonderful to be able to use multiple colors and/or the yellow *Zinnia* to convey the various sentiments desired. Again, the versatility of the language of flowers is advantageous when we are designing these spaces of specific motifs.

- Loveage is a wonderful kitchen herb which lends celery-like flavor to soups, salads, poultry, potatoes, rice, and many other dishes. It is a beautiful plant to grow in pots, as I have illustrated in the sentiment garden, and it is cold hardy down to -5°F. The flowers are charming, with flat umbels of tiny yellowish-white colors in profusion. This sweet herb is a win on many levels, and the bees especially love it!

- If you grow Johnny-jump-ups in pots, they will end up on the ground all around it in the next year. If you grow Johnny-jump-ups in the ground, they will end up in some pots too! That's how it goes with this incredibly profuse little plant. So many seeds dispersed, and an amazingly simple germination process equals proliferation!

> "Flowers may well have provided our remote ancestors with the first consoling narrative. When self-consciousness emerged in human prehistory, it brought with it an experience of separation and an awareness of mortality. These existential predicaments have been with us ever since, raising age-old questions: How to make sense of life? How to deal with the pain that comes from living?
>
> The life of a flower offers something to hold on to, a form of protection against fears of fragmentation in the face of death. Ephemeral and fragile as flowers are, they are the agents of continuity. For the flower in its beauty is destined to die so that its fruit may live and bring forth more flowers from its seed."
>
> —SUE STUART SMITH,
> The Well Gardened Mind
>
> *Reprinted by permission of HarperCollins Publishers Ltd © 2020 by Sue Stuart Smith*

FRIENDS AND FLOWERS

We have used flowers for thousands of years to commemorate milestones, celebrate events, and honor our loved ones in the various seasons of life. So, it is only fitting and appropriate that we use them to nurture and commend our sisterhood and brotherhood relationships too. And in this case, a friendship posy or other floriography gift reminds us that these relationships offer the loyal companionship we crave as humans, and they encapsulate simple and lovely things too, all wrapped in a package of overall joy, beauty, and feel-good vibes. It is wonderful to be a friend, and it is wonderful to have a friend, and there is no better way to communicate the feeling of friendship than with flowers.

THE FRIENDS AND FLOWERS FLORIOGRAPHY GARDEN & FRIENDSHIP POSY

Just as a garden and its flowers require a little tending now and then, our friendships also benefit from a bit of nurturing to keep things flourishing. A gift from a *Friends and Flowers Floriography Garden* is just what is needed to keep things happy, rewarding, and vibrant in our friendships. Whether you snip a few blooms for a sweet en masse bouquet or composition, or you create a complex and lush posy, you will be pleased as punch when you present this to a bestie, and they will never forget the gesture either.

THE *Friends & Flowers* FLORIOGRAPHY GARDEN

- *Alstroemeria* (aka **Peruvian lily, Inca lily**): friendships, powerful bond
- **Catmint** (*Nepeta mussinii*): spirited, good-natured, I want to have fun!
- *Gaura** (*Oenothe*, aka **Siskiyou pink, bee blossom, wand flower**): exhilarating, refreshing personality
- **Geranium, oak-leaf** (*Pelargonium quercifolium*): design to smile, true friendship++
- *Grevillea:* loyalty, steadfastness, impulsive acts of love++
- **Horehound:** virtue, health++
- *Hydrangea:* courageous woman+
- **Ivy leaf:** friendship
- **Orchid, all varieties:** love, thoughtfulness, rare beauty

ALTERNATE AND SEASONAL *Variations*

- **Almond tree:** abiding love and friendship, giddiness, hope, wisdom++
- **Blue chalk sticks*** (*Senecio* succulent species, aka string of bananas, string of pearls): companionship, harmony, understanding, engaging conversations, curiosity, occasionally spicy personality
- **Buttonbush** (*Cephalanthus occidentalis*, aka button willow): cherished friendship
- *Ceanothus:* vibrant personality
- *Chrysanthemum,* **bronze color:** joy, long life, truth, friendship ++
- **Jade** (*Crassula ovata,* aka money plant, friendship tree): affluence, friendship, good luck, money, health, happiness++
- **Moonwort** (aka *Lunaria,* money plant): honesty, fascination, sincerity++
- **Mossy saxifrage** (*Saxifraga,* aka rockfoil): affection
- **Peppermint:** warmth of feeling, cordiality
- **Rose, yellow color:** friendship

What a wonderful way to celebrate friendships, recognize their accomplishments, or just to share your bountiful, beautiful garden! A *Friendship Posy* shows that you care for your friends and that you cherish your relationships with them. This posy is filled with the sentiments and meanings that are not often conveyed in our friendships but certainly should be.

FRIENDS AND FLOWERS GARDENS AND POSIES

THE SENTIMENTS OF GOODWILL AND FELLOWSHIP GARDEN

Gathering with friends or being alone in a *Goodwill and Fellowship Garden* is all you need to feed the soul, share some laughs, or provide support and sustenance to one another. A sense of community among our friends is cherished and loved, and our friendships are one of the most fulfilling relationships we have as humans. How lovely to sit amid the trees and flowers and relish in goodwill and fellowship!

THE SENTIMENTS OF *Goodwill & Fellowship* GARDEN

- *Ajuga* (aka bugle): most loveable, cheers the heart
- **Hyacinth, blue color:** constancy, given to departing friends
- *Iris* (aka fleur-de-lis): ardor, faith, valued friendship
- **Pear blossom:** lasting friendship, affections, more than just lovely
- **Snowdrops** (*Galanthus*): support, consolation, hope, a friend in adversity
- **Virginia sweetspire*** (*Itea virginica,* aka sweetspire): you radiate kindness, dazzling personality

Garden Notes

- Catmint, *Nepeta mussinii*, is a wonderful addition to any garden, be it in the ground or in pots. I adore it! I plant some almost yearly and usually place them around the base of the roses in the rose garden. They are so charming as soft edging and border plant, too, because they stay tidy and don't lose their delicate rounded shape. The bees and other pollinators love them, and of course, so do a couple of my kitties.

- If you plant ivy in your garden, consider installing root barriers around them at planting time to prevent it from taking over the whole place in the future. If left untamed, it will quickly run up walls, trees, benches—really anything. It also chokes out the other plants in the vicinity with their running roots and will deplete the soil of nitrogen and other nutrients. I love having ivy in the garden. I mean, who doesn't? It is classic and timeless, but it must be controlled.

- *Lunaria*, also known as honesty, money plant, moneywort, is one of the most intriguing and fun annuals to grow. They are reliable, self-seeding, incredibly hardy, and so rewarding through all phases of their life, every year! I have a scattering of them on the edge of the woods that I have admired since I arrived at this property thirty-eight years ago. Just like clockwork, they spring up late winter, throw a show of brilliant purple flowers throughout the summer, and then present the glorious papery, silvery, *money* seed pods in the fall. I simply cannot imagine this place without them. I adore bringing those seed pods into the house in the fall. Once they have become iridescent, they are gloriously beautiful in autumn posies!

Empowerment and Ambition

There are few things in this world that can instill a sense of worth, pride, and get-up-and-go like a bunch of gorgeous blooms can—especially when they are gifted to us in such a manner that the blooms do the talking. It is a tall order to make someone feel like they can bootstrap it and keep trudging through tough times, gather the bravery and strength to do something very scary, or even just keep getting up in the morning under dire circumstances. Inevitably, from time to time, we will all need the power of flowers!

THE EMPOWERMENT AND AMBITION FLORIOGRAPHY GARDEN & UNIQUELY YOU POSY

This lovely garden is another wonderful example of how versatile and useful the language of flowers can be. As you can see in the *Uniquely You Posy*, if you use all six of the plants and flowers featured, it creates an exquisite composition. On the other hand, can you imagine how gorgeous a bud vase of a single trailing *Clematis* bloom for **mental beauty, artfulness**, and **ingenuity** would be? Or a lovely en masse gathering of porcelina roses for **admiration**? And in addition to this garden, there are copious amounts of flowers and plants that convey empowerment, uniqueness, and ambition. The possibilities are endless, and what a thoughtful, uplifting gesture to give away some of these incredible, strengthening thoughts and feelings to another person.

THE *Empowerment & Ambition* FLORIOGRAPHY GARDEN

- ***Clematis*** (aka old man's beard, traveler's joy, virgin's bower): mental beauty, artfulness, soul mates ++
- **Vervain (*Verbena*)**: faithfulness, sensibility, enchantment
- **Indian pink, single (*Dianthus chinensis*)**: you are aspiring, always lovely ++
- **Porcelina rose**: admiration
- **Rosemary**: wisdom, intellect, your presence refreshes ++
- **Smoke bush (*Cotinus coggygria*, aka Venetian sumac, smoke tree)**: generous in spirit, radiant and dreamy, intellectual excellence, splendor++

ALTERNATE AND SEASONAL *Variations*

- *Angelica:* inspiration, magic, symbol of poetic inspiration++
- *Campanula* (aka bellflower): aspiring, without pretention++
- *Brodiaea* (aka cluster-lilies, fool's onion): cultured, intellect, heartfelt, poetic, creative soul
- Darling pea* (*Swainsonia*): resilient, graceful beauty, a lady in every way++
- Peppermint geranium (*Pelargonium tomentosum*, aka peppermint-scented geranium): invigoration, inspiration ++
- *Ginkgo biloba* (aka maidenhair tree): longevity, solitary beauty, enlightenment, profound endurance, thoughtfulness
- Primrose, lilac color (*Primula, P. polyantha*, aka polyanthus primrose—with clusters of flowers on one stem—false oxlip): confidence, elegance, the heart's mystery ++
- Rice flower*: longevity, richness, abundance++
- Water lily: beauty, purity of heart, wisdom, soothing, harmony++
- *Watsonia* (aka bugle lily): harmony, inspiration, stability

We all have moments and feelings of less-than-perfect inadequacies, and couple that with the peaks and valleys we all go through in life, which can take a toll on us, and can even be detrimental to our happiness. As I have said before, flowers make us happy, and these blooms, with their cherished thoughts and messages, are a surefire way to tell someone that they really are *all that*, and a lot more. Receiving a posy like this is certain to bring to light our beautiful uniqueness and highlight our strength and power. It is a favorite of mine, as I love being able to uplift my family and friends with sentiments that simply cannot be conveyed with words or actions. It must be this posy!

EMPOWERMENT AND AMBITION GARDENS AND POSIES

THE INTENT AND ASPIRATIONS SENTIMENT GARDEN

Some flowers and plants require only that you just set eyes upon them—in all their perfection and diversity—silky, feathery greens, luminous buds, and spiraled rosettes, allowing us to gain momentum with our intentions and fuel our aspirations. Our gardens—no matter the planting scheme, no matter how many blooms you have, or how big or small, can lift us up better than anything else.

THE *Intent & Aspirations* SENTIMENT GARDEN

- *Aeonium:* long life, vivacity, resilience
- *Grevillea:* loyalty, intent, diversity++
- **Mountain ash (*Sorbus L.*, aka rowan):** ambition, healing, empowerment, protection, balance, transformation++
- **Sage:** great wisdom and respect, esteem, strength ++
- **Silver fir (*Abies alba, Abies amabilis*):** what you seek shall be found
- **Tiger lily:** majesty, honor, purity of heart, pride++

Garden Notes

- Historically, the silver fir was the first species used as Christmas trees in Europe. Silver firs come in numerous shapes and sizes and can be suitable for any sort of garden or landscape. Not to be confused with Douglas firs, *Pseudotsuga menziesii* (not a true fir), the silver fir, or *Abies alba*, along with other true firs, have cylindrical cones that grow erect on the branch, pointing upward, and will disintegrate before falling to the ground. On the contrary, the Douglas fir cones hang downward from the branch and fall to the ground intact.

- Why are we not all growing water lilies? They are incredibly easy to grow, and you do not need a pond. They only need a depth of 12 to 16 inches from the bottom, so a large pot or tub set on your patio will do fine. There are many colors available, but the hardy varieties are usually pastel tones, whereas the tropical varieties will be brighter jewel tones. With the symbolisms of **beauty, purity of the heart**, and **wisdom**, they are a profound messenger and gift from the garden and enriched with unmatched history of our spirit and humanity.

PART 3
How to Arrange
Posies and Bouquets

After twenty-five-plus years (and counting!) of floristry, I can say without hesitation that I know a few things about growing and arranging flowers. And I am honored and happy to share my expertise and experience with you here. Just as in *The Posy Book,* I have summarized all the information to include only the most essential, practical, and supportive methods of flower arranging and crafting posies. I'm including simple facts that can't be argued, and the emphasis is on ***simple***. But they are valuable, and they've taken me many years to master and perfect. By applying a few techniques, you will develop an acquaintance with the flowers and other materials, gain new perspectives, and of course, feel confident in your floral design endeavors. Cultivating flowers and plants, and then taking that lovely thing that you grew or acquired and turning it into beautiful, heartfelt, and memorable gifts will leave you with a warm feeling of triumph. It really does feel good to craft something with your own hands, and it gives the gift such added depth and appreciation.

Gathering *and Preparation*

When selecting your materials for a gift of floriography, whether it is for a posy or a simple gathering of a single type of branch or bloom, or a stunning en masse arrangement, you must begin by considering the occasion, message, or sentiment you want to convey. Often, the garden's available resources will determine your overall message, or an impromptu splurge of market-bought flowers will direct the sentiment as well. It has happened to me more times than I can count, where I have purchased an exquisite bunch of flowers and let those flowers spark or lead the message to myself (self-care!) or for a gift to another person. To assist you in determining the overall message of your floriography gifts, review the handy "Quick-Start Directories" in part 5. And remember, when creating a posy or for any form of floriography, you can use all parts of the plant to convey its messages in the language of flowers, unless there are specific meanings for the individual parts, such as the berries or the fruit.

Regardless, the materials you use need to be prepped and ready for the presentation and to live its best, longest, and most beautiful life outside its natural environment. Once flowers are cut, they begin the process of deterioration, so it is important to push out that process as long as possible. And you can do that by prepping and caring for them promptly and properly once they are in your hands.

Harvesting and Conditioning

When harvesting flowers from the garden, I recommend always cutting flowers in the morning so that the midday sun or other environmental stressors are at their lowest, and the blooms are at their healthiest and most hydrated state. Once a flower is cut from the plant, their life begins to end. Therefore, to give them the best potential as a cut flower, here are some tips:

❋ Carry a bucket of water with you while cutting and harvesting your materials. Once you have cut the flower or greenery, remove any leaves down the stem that will not be used as part of your design. Place the stripped and cleaned stem in the bucket immediately, so that they can begin to draw water without delay to where you need it—the blooms, or the top leaves. The stripped-off leaves can simply be dropped at the base of the plant you've just cut from, and they will compost right back into the plant it came from, with the exact nutrients it needs. Pretty nifty, right?

❋ The following flowers tend to be grumpy straightaway after the cut, so save them for last so that they spend less time in the garden and can be transported quickly to a cool place: *Hydrangea*, garden roses, hellebore, and any delicate, single, thin-petaled perennials such as geum, cosmos, tweedia, and tender herbs such as mint or lemon balm, and the fuzzy-leafed, scented *Pelargoniums*. In fact, through the years, I have learned to submerse the entire scented *Pelargonium* leaves—the ones that I'll use in my design, down into the bucket of water as I go so that those leaf surface cells can hydrate by transpiration—meaning water is absorbed into the leaf's cells, and this usually will prevent them from suffering wilted leaves. Just make sure the end of the stems where you cut are also submerged, because you don't want that end cut exposed to air. This method of submersion-hydration also applies to dusty miller, grape leaves, *Begonia*, and other leaves that have porous, non-shiny surfaces.

❋ *Dahlias* love to be placed immediately into a bucket of hot water after they're cut, and the leaves and side shoot blooms have been removed. This means you will need a separate harvest bucket for the *Dahlias*, as the other blooms won't appreciate a hot water bath. The water should be hot to the touch, but not boiling. The hot water opens the stem cells and allows them to hydrate their petals easier and faster. Basically, it keeps those cells wide open for water transportation straight up to the petals, which is where you want it. After a 15-minute soak in hot water, move them into room temperature water with commercial flower food. Store them as cool as possible, and if you have refrigeration, that is best. The large, decorative or dinnerplate varieties are the most challenging to keep from petal-flopping, and this hot-water method, coupled with refrigeration, is their best chance at longevity. For this reason, the best varieties for vase life as cut flowers are the pompon, ball, and some of the cactus varieties, as they do not have large floppy petals, and their size and composition work best in posies too.

❁ Some flowers and plant materials have toxic milky sap housed in their stems. This sap causes rapid deterioration to other flowers and plant materials if you place them into the same bucket of water after cutting. Always place milky sap flowers in a separate bucket to allow them to leak and drain out the sap before you combine them with other plant materials in water. This same milky sap can also cause skin dermatitis, which is why I always recommend using disposable gloves while working with these flowers and plants. And finally, they are also toxic when ingested, so please use extreme caution if you have pets:

- ✓ Daffodils, including *Narcissus*
- ✓ *Euphorbias* and spurges
- ✓ Milkweeds, including the dogbane cousin, *Oxypetalum coeruleum,* aka tweedia
- ✓ Poppies (you can sear their stems at the cut to seal and prevent the milk-sap leak)
- ✓ Oleanders (I do not recommend cutting oleanders for ornamental use. These plants are just too toxic and not meant for these purposes. Besides, look at what they mean in the language of flowers; **beware, caution, danger, distrust**)
- ✓ Periwinkle, *Vinca minor*
- ✓ Plumeria
- ✓ Daphne
- ✓ Agapanthus

And there are certainly more that I am not aware of.

❁ When cutting flowers from a garden plant, where and how you place the cut on the plant is important, and sometimes detrimental to its health, growth habits, and even future flowers. This varies depending on what the variety or genus is and the growth habit of the plant. But, in general you want to always cut above a node. And the node that you select to cut from, whether it is outward facing, or inward facing determines the future shape and health of the plant.

HOW TO ARRANGE POSIES AND BOUQUETS

Using a rosebush as an example, always cut above an outward node. This will prompt new outward growth. Roses need air circulation throughout the bush to prevent disease. By leaving open space inside the plant, you will reduce the chance of mildew and other airborne diseases. Clean and sharp clippers are necessary. It is highly probable that you spread disease from plant to plant with dirty clippers!

❀ There are flowers that bloom only on old wood, and some that bloom only on new wood. Determining which one you have will depend on its primary bloom time. In general, plants that bloom in the spring set their blooms on old wood, and plants that bloom in the summer and fall set their blooms on new wood. When harvesting your flowers, be sure to keep in mind that if you cut into woody stems, you may be removing next year's bloom. Typical examples of these plants and flowers are *Hydrangea*s, *Clematis* (there are both spring bloomers and summer/fall bloomers), *Deutzia*, and lilac, to name a few. When pruning these after their spring flush of blooms, always cut just above the first set of nodes below the spent bloom, thereby assuring you are not cutting into next year's bloom set. On the contrary, if you have a plant that is blooming on new growth, then you really don't have much to worry about unless you are overharvesting in the spring. And if you unknowingly remove its bud set, then some varieties will send out additional blooms for you to enjoy later into the summer.

- When cutting *Hydrangea*, hellebore, and all the mint family, including *Coleus*, the age of the stem and bloom is a critical indicator of the life of the cut flower. These types of flowers do not hold up well when they are cut too soon. In the case of *Hydrangea*, if you cut the blooms when they're too young on the bush—meaning fully bloomed-out for less for than one or two weeks, then more likely their heavy heads will flop and wilt. You want to cut *Hydrangea*s and mints when they are at the *going woody state*, meaning that there are subtle blotches of dark brown running up and down the green stem. If you see this, it is probably a good time to cut as it indicates the cells are hardening and, as a result, are becoming sturdier—woody, and have the ability to retain water better. And in the case of hellebore, try to cut mature blooms by noting the stamens in the center. If the stamens have dropped, you have a mature bloom and thus, will last much longer than a younger bloom with lots of fresh stamens. Even with this method of timing your cuts, sometimes these plants will still flop, as they are very sensitive to air in their stems. You can usually revive a wilted *Hydrangea* or stem of mint by submersing the entire stem, including the head on the *Hydrangea*, into a bucket of room temperature water and let them hydrate there for 15 minutes. Always be sure that you have submerged the cut end of the stem, too, as you don't want it exposed to air. After soaking, recut the stems and set them back into the water—stem-down this time, and keep them in a cool area. They should come back to life within an hour. Additionally, for hellebore, add a slit up the length of the stem, stopping almost at the head of the flower. Cut just deep enough that water can penetrate the stem through the slit, being cautious not to cut all the way through. This method simply opens more cells in the stem for uptake.

Properly conditioning your flowers is undoubtedly the most important step in providing the best chance for a long and beautiful vase life. The following information applies to both store-bought flowers and garden grown flowers.

- First, remove unwanted leaf material. Unless the leaves are part of your message in floriography, we do not want them on the stem. Removing all the leaves—all the way up to the bloom enables the water to travel up the stem and directly to the bloom, rather than to the leaves. Clearing the stems of leaves like this also prevents underwater leaf material from rotting and decaying. If you are cutting from the garden, you will have already removed most of the leaf material as you were cutting them, but a quick check for any additional leaf material is necessary.

- Recut the stems on both garden cuts and store-bought just prior to placing them into a container of clean, room temperature water and flower food. Stems should be cut at a sharp angle, which provides a larger surface area to uptake water.

- Woody stemmed flowers such as lilacs need more than just a cut and set into water. Their stems are too hardened to drink efficiently and the blossom on top will suffer and flop right way. You need to help them hydrate, and to do this you should make two 1-inch-long vertical snips up from the bottom of the stem to open more area for water uptake. These cuts should be opposite sides of the stem from one another. I do not recommend hammering or beating the bottom of the stem to fray it, as this may cause cellular damage and can result in clogging the stem and preventing water uptake. I have always used the slit method, and it works nicely.

- If you are not using your flowers immediately, you will need to ensure that they are stored in a cool place, out of any warming sunlight or other heat sources. If you have refrigeration, then of course use it because it is beneficial to keep the flowers as cool as possible to slow the deterioration of your blooms. However, keep in mind that it is not a good idea for flowers to share refrigeration with fruit and vegetables for long periods, as they emit ethylene gas, which deteriorates the blooms very quickly, and compromises the overall health of the cut flowers. Rather than sharing the fridge with fruits and veggies, it would be best to just try and keep them happy and as cool as possible by keeping their bucket water on the cold side.

Methods *and Instructions*

Please see the *Resource Directory* for all tools and supplies used and suggested in the following methods.

Posy Perfection and the Characteristics of Good Floral Design

Posies are floral arrangements that measure approximately 7 to 12 inches in diameter. Because of their petite stature, it is required that we follow guidelines to assure your posy imparts an elegant composition that is aesthetically appealing to the eye and lends a beautiful enhancement to any environment. Some of the guidelines are taken directly from my golden rule book of standard floral design, but some, as outlined here, are meant to be applied specifically to the design of posies.

- **Balanced textures.** There should be only 1 or 2 types of greens that have coarse, strong textures so as not to dominate the posy. The deeply lobed leaves of some *Pelargoniums,* some varieties of ferns such as sword and leatherleaf, and most varieties of ninebark are a few examples of coarse textures. Try to use these coarse textures in balance with some greens and herbs of smooth and subtle textures, such as dusty miller, lamb's ear, and licorice (*Helichrysum*).
- **Balanced flower types**. Some flowers have a lot of texture and complex parts, and some are smooth and simple. Try to bring both types into your arrangement to complement one another. For instance, if you use pincushion *Protea*, which is a strong and complex flower, along with another flower that has a profusion of flowers on the stem, such as *Eriostemon* or wax flower, you will lose your balanced aesthetic, and the arrangement will impart a messy and weedy feeling. So, if you use a flower such as a pincushion *Protea* or a peony, both strong and complex, then your

complementary flowers should be subtly smooth and uncomplicated, such as a sweetheart rose, cosmos, or geum, for example.

- **Focal flowers.** Defined as *mass* and *form* flowers, focal flowers are used to create the shape and outline in a posy. Usually, we use anywhere from 3 to 7 stems, depending upon the size of the focal flowers.

Some examples of focal flowers are Roses, *Chrysanthemum*s, and *Hydrangea*s. In the case of the *Hydrangea*, which is typically used as a semi-focal flower because of its umbel-type blooms, where the umbel is comprised of many small florets, it would need other focal flowers inserted into these umbels. Usually only one or two stems are needed because they are large-headed flowers that fill up space quickly.

Roses

Hydrangea

Chrysanthemum

- ❋ **Complementary flowers.** Sometimes referred to as *fillers* in the floral industry, but in posies, complementary flowers are an integral part of the posy's story. In addition, their role in the design is to enhance the focal flowers, herbs, and greenery. Usually approximately 5 to 7 stems work well, but of course, depending on the types and how large they are.

A few examples of complementary flowers are solidaster, snapdragons, and Queen Anne's lace. Discoid shaped flowers such as Queen Anne's lace, *Scabiosas*, and tender-stemmed cluster flowers such as *Narcissus* and primrose will need stem and bloom support inside the posy. Do this by laying them up against or tucking them in next stronger-stemmed companions in the posy.

'*Solidago* aka solidaster'

Snapdragons

Queen Anne's Lace

- ❁ **Necklace greenery.** In the world of floriography, foliage and greens are heavy hitters, and *Pelargoniums*, and specifically the fancy and scented-leaf varieties are the all-star players. They are used in posies as *necklace greens*, because, when placed around the outside edge of the posies, they create a delicate and beautiful frame for the entire composition. There are many types of greens and herbs that will do this as well as the geranium, such as dusty miller and *Pittosporum*. Usually, you will need 5 to 7 stems of necklace greens, but again, it will depend upon their individual sizes and volume.

'*Pelargonium* aka geranium'

Dusty Miller

Pittosporum

- ❁ **Agreeable colors.** Using a color wheel as an example, a monochromatic or analogous color theme will always elevate your design to a more formal composition. Using complementary colors will do this as well and will also impart more whimsy.

- ❁ **Overall design principle.** I do love the big, wild, and showy floral designs, and I am certainly partial to what I call *circus bouquets*, which are fun, flirty, and uninhibited floral designs that knock your socks off. However, this is a posy—an intimate gathering of flowers that will convey delicate and sometimes sensitive messages to the beneficiaries. For this reason, the overall aesthetic should carry a level of formality. And if the sentiments of your posy allow, it is suitable to lend some fun and whimsy into it too. Either way, since posies are generally petite, we need to keep things designed in pavé style, which means flowers, herbs, or greens are not protruding from the top of the design. The finished posy should be mostly smooth, as the name pavé implies, a paving of its elements laid in an orderly fashion. This type of design also gives a nod of respect to the history and the origins of the posy, being very intricately formatted, and designed with great organization and placement of the flowers.

Selecting Your Container

It is important to have your vase selected prior to starting on your posy. You don't want to have your finished posy sitting outside of a water source while selecting the perfect container. My absolute favorite containers for posies are water or wine goblets. Their sizes range, but most are 8 inches high, with 3- to 3.5-inch openings. The reason I favor this type of stemware container is because it allows your sentiment tag with ribbons to be displayed vertically, hanging down freely and unencumbered from the edge of the posy, allowing you to highlight your thoughtfully curated gift in a unique and beautiful way. But there are things I like about other containers too, such as footed dessert dishes—again, they have feet that serve to elevate and highlight your sentiment tag. However, a vintage mint julep cup is also a stunner with a gorgeous posy in it, and the sentiment tag is just as lovely in front of the metallic surface of the vessel. Really, anything you desire would work, but keep in mind that the size of the posy and your container should be appropriate. For example, generally the container should be anywhere from 6 to 10 inches in height, and the opening should be no less than 3 inches and no bigger than 4.

As seen here, containers that work beautifully for posies are varied, but they are all of the statures that work best for the size of the posy.

It is vitally important that you have all your conditioned and prepped botanic materials, along with the following materials, laid out in front of you prior to creating your posy. This allows you to focus only on the formation of your posy in hand, rather than breaking out to collect needed items.

MATERIALS NEEDED
to Make a Posy

- All botanical elements, prepped and conditioned, with stem lengths trimmed to approximately 12"
- Garden or hemp twine precut to a length of 12"
- Sharp, clean scissors and gardening snips or any straight-blade clipper with a narrow end to get into tight spaces
- Your selected posy vessel, vase, or container filled with room temperature water with a pinch of commercial flower food mixed in

HOW TO ARRANGE POSIES AND BOUQUETS

Ready, Set, Go!

Posies are constructed from the inside going outward, and in a centrifugal manner. An easy way to start your posy is by beginning with a focal flower. In this case, I am using a rose as my focal flower, and a *Hydrangea* as a semi-focal flower. The *Hydrangea* is a large umbel-type flower, so they work well to tuck other flowers into the center, from the top. If you are not using *Hydrangea* as one of your focal flowers, it's OK; just start with your chosen focal and build outward as instructed and shown below.

Next, create a central pivot by adding two or three stems of complementary flowers right around it. You can then add one or two sprigs of an herb tucked in around that. This central pivot will now be the very middle and center of your posy and you can begin to build the posy outward.

You do this by adding another focal flower, some complementary flowers, herbs—and if you've got any fun enhancement materials such as berries, cotton, or seed pods, add those into the posy at this point. Keep building outward until you've reached its appropriate diameter of approximately 9 inches. If you're new at this, you might find yourself squeezing or gripping the posy tightly at this point because it could all fall apart, right? But try to keep a loose yet firm hold on it and practice turning it clockwise in your hand so that you can observe the placement of your materials better. You want to ensure all your focal flowers are equally distanced where complementary flowers aren't all bunched together, and so on.

Finally, add your necklace greens around the edges, and that should be the final *voila!*

Tie off your posy using the *grower's tie* method.

Lay the twine across the posy as high up and underneath the necklace greens as possible, leaving one endpiece about 5 inches long, and wrapping the other end twice around the base of the posy, meeting the two ends of twine together. Gently squeeze—you want to tie the ends together tightly, but not so tight that the stems cannot pull up water. Use your scissors to snip off the tails of the twine. *See images 9 and 10 on the next page as well.*

Next, depending on the depth of the vessel you've chosen to use, cut the stems off enough to allow the posy to sit on its collar around the top edge of the vase. The stems should not be touching the bottom of the container, rather the posy should be resting on the rim of the container.

Besides adding flair and beauty to a posy or bouquet, ribbons are necessary in order to attach and hold the sentiment tags onto the gift you will be presenting. Of course, there are other ways to attach your sentiment tags to your posy, such as with string or twine, and that's just fine too. But ribbons add color, texture, elegance, and sometimes whimsy to your designs, depending on the style you choose. It's all up to you. Following is a list of materials you will need to create two different styles of ribbon adornment for your posy: tab-style, and bow-style. Both styles allow you to attach the sentiment tag to the tail of the ribbon.

MATERIALS NEEDED TO CONSTRUCT
Ribbon Adornment

- Ribbon or ribbons of your choice, widths ranging from ¾" up to 2"
- Sharp scissors
- 24-gauge precut, straight floral wire, approximately 6" long
- 4" unwired wooden floral stick

TAB-STYLE RIBBON DIRECTIONS

Start by cutting two (or three!) color-coordinated ribbons at varying lengths of 12", 14", and if desired, 16". Of course, you can always use just one ribbon, too, but the width of the ribbon should be no more than 2". Otherwise, you will not be able to run it through the punched hole on the sentiment tag.

Make a loop midway down the length of the ribbons.

Lay the floral wire across the bottom of the loop. Draw both ends of the wire together at the back and then twist them together as tightly as possible. The tighter the twist, the fluffier the tab!

Now you can twist the already twisted wire ends down the wooden stick.

HOW TO ARRANGE POSIES AND BOUQUETS

This stick is what you place in the front of your posy by tucking it directly behind the tied-twine binding of the posy itself.

LAYERED, DOUBLE BOW-STYLE RIBBON DIRECTIONS

Start by cutting two color-coordinated 32" long swaths of ribbon. One ribbon should be ¾" and the other should be 1–2" wide. Simply lay the narrower ribbon on top of the wider ribbon, then proceed to the next step.

Approximately 6" from the ribbon end, make a 5" loop. Do another loop, the same size, on the opposite side of the first one. Repeat this until you have made four loops total, two on each side. Keep your fingers in the center of these loops, holding the ribbon layers and loops snugly at this central point. You should have two tails of ribbon hanging, roughly the same length.

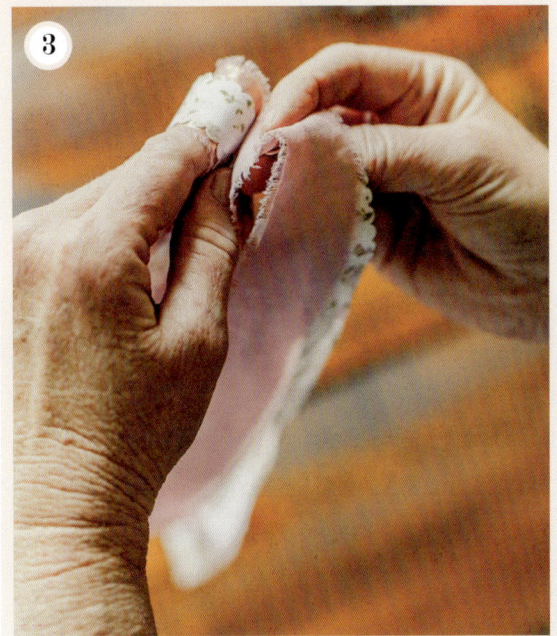

Bind the ribbons together by placing the floral wire vertically across the central point where the ribbon loops are even on both sides.

HOW TO ARRANGE POSIES AND BOUQUETS

Squeeze the wire together tightly, while holding the loops out of the way, and upward in the other hand. Squeeze so tight and twist the legs of the wire all the way down. Secure the wire onto a green stick by placing the wire at the top of the stick and then twist it all the way down. Now, you have a sturdy way to stick the bow down into the binding on the posy.

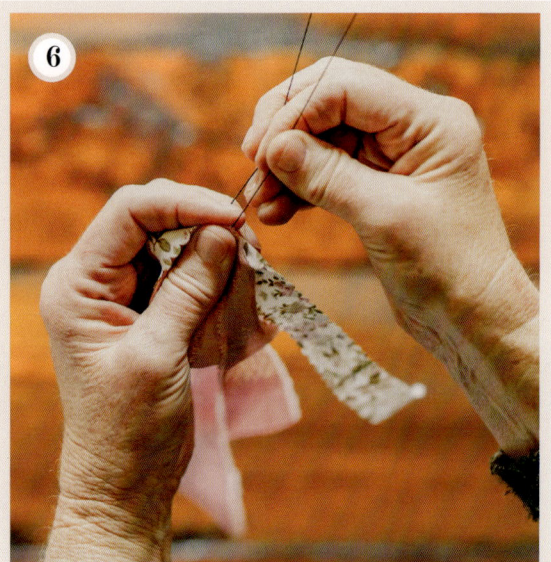

SENTIMENT TAGS

In addition to the beauty of your gifts of flowers and plants, the sentiment tags that are attached are just as much loved and adored and are a vitally important part of the gift. A sentiment tag is a note that is attached to your gift of floriography that deciphers the flowers and their meanings. Regardless of whether your gift is a posy, a bouquet, or a live plant, it must include a sentiment tag—without them, while your gifts would still be gorgeous, they would not be understood as anything other than a beautiful bunch of flowers or a lovely plant. Unless your recipients are floriographers themselves, they will have no way of recognizing the gift's numerous heartfelt sentiments that are being imparted to them.

Sentiment tags can be made in the simplest fashion or in very ritzy and elaborate ways. After the flowers have waned, the tag and its intricate and intimate story is what the recipient often holds on to in one way or another as a touching memento of your thoughtfulness.

There are no strict guidelines that you need to follow regarding the design of your sentiment tag. It is an incredibly thoughtful process, and creating these beautiful tokens can be a lively crafting experience with glitter, baubles, medallions . . . you name it. Or it can be a simple, minimally decorated, handwritten note on pretty paper. Traditionally, the sentiment tag should measure about 2.5 inches wide and 3.5 inches long. This enables the tag to be small enough to attach to posies and other petite presentations, and large enough to be read clearly by the recipient and allows space for any embellishment.

There are ready-to-go sentiment tags available for download from my website, **teresasabankaya.com**. You have two choices of format for downloading: Word or PDF, and there are several sets of tags that are complementary and some that are slightly more elaborate for purchase, as well as floriography tags for en masse bouquets. Either way, just download them and then fill in the flower names and their meanings along with your personal message on the back, if desired. If you want to make your own tags, the options are literally endless. I suggest using the graphic design website **Canva.com**—it is very user-friendly and offers limitless design elements from simple to very elaborate design options.

Card stock papers are available in plenty of colors and patterns, but through the many years that I have been making sentiment tags, my preference is a medium-weight white card stock for the sentiment tags. The fun graphic prints, elegant toiles, and beautifully textured papers are what I love to use as backing on the tags. In this case, the fronts and backs of the tags will need to be printed on two separate pieces of paper, and the pretty paper placed in between. Also on my website, you can purchase my Sentiment Tag Kits, which are filled with all you will need to jump-start tag-making, which can be shipped nationwide. The kits include several swaths of gorgeous ribbons, a few blank, pre-printed sentiment tags, graphic papers, and some elegant and fun embellishments. See the *Resource Directory* for where to find additional provisions for making sentiment tags.

Here are just a few examples of how beautiful and fun sentiment tags can be. The choice is yours, so get tag crafting!

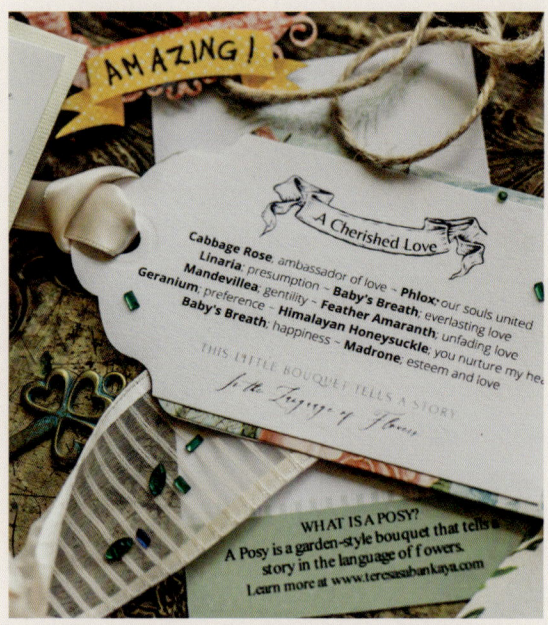

Bountiful Bouquets

As described in part 1, en masse bouquets are meant to be used as messengers of one set of sentiments of one specific flower or other botanic. Because we use only one type of bloom, the arrangement of these bouquets can be quite simple. Other times, we can make them a bit more elaborate in their design and compositions and this applies also to their packaging, decorations, and embellishments. It is enjoyable to match blooms, branches, leaves, and various textures of nature to beautiful papers and textiles. What makes these bouquet gifts memorable is not only the flowers themselves but also the effort you put into enhancing their natural beauty with your own special crafting.

To begin, you will use the same techniques and guidelines for harvesting or acquiring your flowers, except there's no need to cut the stems down. Just keep the stems at a reasonable length to create a presentation bouquet, which should be in the range of 10 to 16 inches. Of course, it is appropriate to simply leave your bunch as they lay, without any adjustments to their way of being held and presented together, but here I will show you how to enhance the bunch a bit with a little fluff and frill. Below are five different wrapping and presentation styles that work with virtually any bouquet of flowers. Whichever style you choose to wrap your bouquet, they each complement the gift and make it a finished and polished presentation worthy of the highest complements.

SPIRALED TULIPS, THREE WAYS

With tulips, I have used the spiral-laid method. Start by laying one tulip directly in front of you vertically on the table. Lay the next one at a slight angle and a tiny bit lower on either side of the first one. Repeat this process, alternating sides, and paying attention to where the stems cross over one another, assuring that they are at the same point, until you have the entire bunch laid down. Gather the bunch up into your hand by grabbing around the central crossover point. That is where you tie the bunch off using the grower tie method.

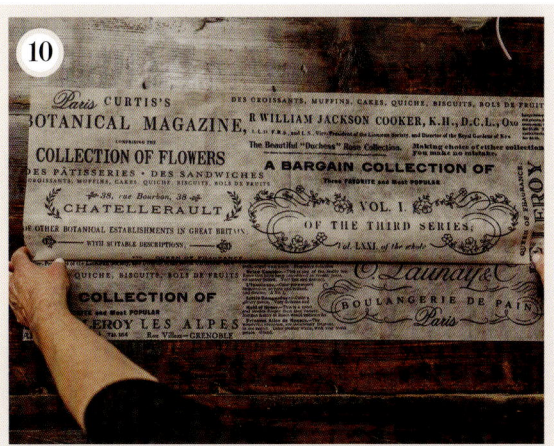

Enter the world of decoupage tissue paper and get ready to unleash your creativity. There are an abundance of patterns, styles, and colors available, and here is a beautiful way to use them.

Begin by laying the paper on a flat surface, in a horizontal direction. Fold the paper once, accordion-style, in order to shorten its height. Lay your bunch of flowers vertically onto the paper. Scrunch the paper's edges toward the stems on both sides and then tie it off with ribbon to secure it. Add additional ribbons, cords, or twine as desired to secure the sentiment tag.

Below are more styles of wrapping your bouquets. I've used tulips in these examples, but any type of flowers will benefit from these styles. And, if you love textiles and pretty papers like I do, then this is your gig. Have a blast with it! It's an important job, too, because your wrapping and presentation are the first impressions made when giving flowers, and just imagine receiving one of these stunners as a gift. It's also fun and easy to do, so don't overlook this fundamental part of gifting flowers.

This style of wrapping allows you to hide the mechanics needed to hydrate your stems, which allows for the bouquet to be out of water for several hours. Here, I have used an eco-friendly flower wrap that creates a water reservoir for cut flowers, which I have used for many years to keep posies hydrated for shipping. Otherwise, a wet paper towel bound around the bottom with a rubber band, and then a baggie bound around that will work well, especially when it's just a few hours until the flowers reach their destination. You can find the source for eco-friendly flower wraps in the *Resource Directory*.

Textiles! A square of coveted scrap fabric will do, but there are also other options, such as dinner napkins and hand towels. This style of wrapping is appropriate if you're certain the flowers will be placed into water within a short time, approximately one hour, and that depends on the climate and type of flowers too. Here, I have used my favorite wrapping textile, a gorgeous tea towel that is a match made in heaven for these tulips. The color goes well, and the contrast in the vintage ribbon to the towel and tulips is quite fetching, don't you think?

SOLDIERED ROSES

When I had my retail flower shop, we wrapped many, many rose bouquets. We tried all the methods of wrapping roses for presentation, and then some. The soldier-style always won us over, without a doubt. Because of a hybrid tea rose's composition of a thin-to-medium stem and then a large head that is usually closed-up on top, they will not arrange well without the accompaniment of a lot of other floral or green materials. But they work perfectly lined up in a staggered formation, and this way, they don't fight for space or need to be highlighted as the star of the show, or most importantly, fall out of shape of the arrangement. They simply lay pleasantly in their lineup, waiting to be admired by the recipient!

Begin by laying out your chosen wrapping tissue, 3–4 layers thick. Then, at an angle to the upper corner of the tissue, line up five or more roses straight across it.

Next, lay your second line of roses about ¾" lower and in between the first two heads of roses. Proceed across the line until you've reached the end. There will be one less rose on this line because you are staggering them.

Proceed down to the next lines and continue until you've laid a single rose in between the only two remaining in the previous line.

Finish the presentation by folding up the bottom of the tissue to cover stems and then fold over the sides to meet in the front middle.

HOW TO ARRANGE POSIES AND BOUQUETS

Tie off the bunch gently with a ribbon as shown, and finish with your sentiment tag.

All dressed up! Isn't this a lovely presentation? This arranging style elevates the simply constructed hybrid tea rose to an elegant affair, and just perfect for so many occasions. And remember, the sentiments in the language of flowers for the rose all vary and depend on colors, so take advantage of that and use some lesser-known messages that roses carry, or just use the primary meanings of **love, beauty,** and **friendship**.

SWEET PEAS, POSY-STYLE

When you need to present a gift a little on the sweeter side, a posy-style wrap will do a lovely job of it. Two varying and coordinated types and patterns of paper are used here, which gives the presentation added complexity and interest. Sweet peas are just perfect for this style as the ruffled front facing of the wrap mimics the precious ruffled blooms, making a simply divine offering.

Soft-hued blooms lend themselves perfectly to this posy-style wrapped bouquet that conveys the messages of **departure, goodbye,** and **tender memory,** all of which are appropriate if you were to gift them as a memorial token for a loss of a loved one or pet.

Gather your blooms into a pretty, rounded bunch, then tie off with twine. Cut stems below the tie off to approximately 6–8" long.

HOW TO ARRANGE POSIES AND BOUQUETS

Lay flowers diagonally across selected paper—in this case, I've used floral wrapping paper. Choose a piece of tissue that coordinates in color to your flowers and wrapping paper. Fold this tissue into quarters, horizontally.

Crinkle the folded tissue from the ends inward like an accordion. Place the crinkled tissue on top of the flowers in the middle so that the fluffy tissue edge lays nicely tucked up against the blooms. Lift the bouquet with tissue up and fold up one side of the wrapping paper at a pleasing angle and then lay the flowers on top.

Fold over the other side of the wrapping paper and squeeze both sides together and tie off with ribbon.

Attach your sentiment tag with ribbons and embellishments if desired. The stems in this style are exposed, so you can either hand off the bouquet to its recipient, or you can carefully place the bottoms of the stems in a small jar of water until it's time to give it away.

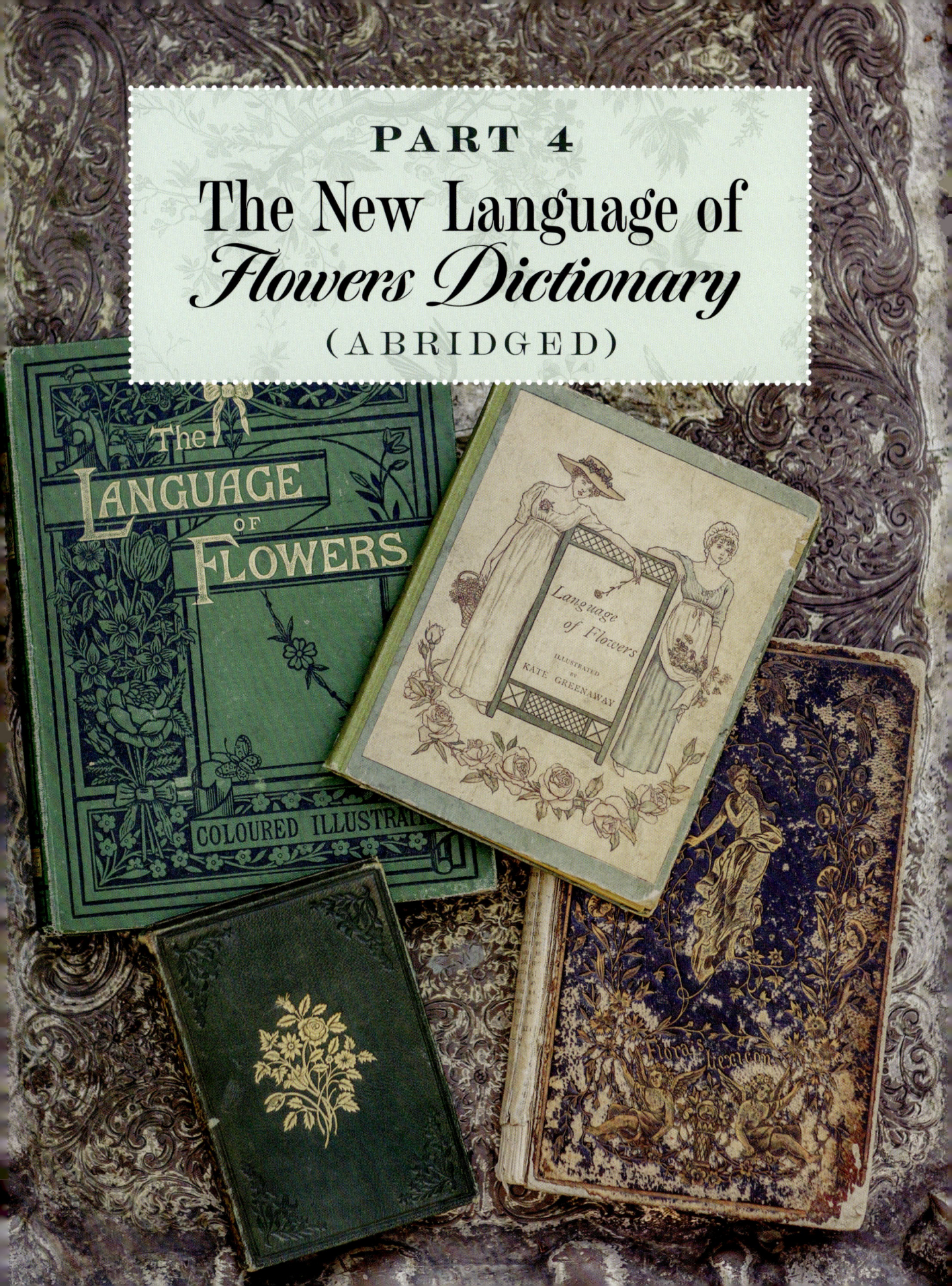

PART 4
The New Language of *Flowers Dictionary*
(ABRIDGED)

The New Language of Flowers

There is a comprehensive floral dictionary in my first book, *The Posy Book*, and if you have that book, then of course you can continue to use that for reference when practicing floriography. The dictionary in this book is an abridged version of that dictionary, and in addition to all the flowers and their meanings referenced throughout this book, includes some of the most common flowers, plants, trees, and herbs for a quick reference. This abridged version also includes several new entries of flowers and plants that, according to my own resources and research, did not have a meaning in the language of flowers, yet they are readily available to use in gardens and floral arrangements. Additionally, there are newly hybridized flowers and plants being introduced on a regular basis, and we want to use these beautiful flowers and plants in floriography. In both cases, as an authority in floriography, with guidance from horticultural professionals and other highly regarded authorities in the language of flowers, I have provided new meanings for these flowers and plants. These meanings are devised and chosen based on several factors, but mainly the plant's genera, species, family, and any common traits they share that may have that distinction reflected in its meaning. Also, the plant's natural habitat: Where does it thrive? What does it not like? Basically, What is the temperament of the plant? That is how flowers and plants have always gotten their connotations and symbolic indicators throughout history, and that is how it should be done now and in the future. This allows us to continue the fundamental purpose of modern floriography, and this book—to be able to utilize most, if not all our plants as messengers in the language of flowers.

Essential Dictionary Notes

✽ The single plus sign (+) denotes that the plant is reflecting its primary meanings, and that there are sub-primary meanings that are not listed here, depending on its color, attributes, and scenarios.

✽ The double plus signs (++) denotes that more definitions are recorded in the comprehensive online dictionary, as noted below.

✽ The asterisks (*) indicates that it is a newly hybridized plant with a new meaning, or an established plant given a meaning for the first time.

✽ Respectfully, a plant's name is written to adhere to the guidelines of horticultural nomenclature. The plant's botanical name is inclusive of the genus, species, and variety, and is always in italics. In most cases, I have listed the most used common name first, but in some instances, the botanical name follows the common name to clarify the variety or genus of the plant. Following that, the plant's common name or names, if they have them, are preceded by "aka," and are not italicized. Not all common names of a plant are noted, as there are too many to include in this book in some cases. I have chosen to include only the ones I believe would be most recognizable to most people. Additionally, the world of botany and horticulture is always evolving, and often plants are reclassified and given new names. I attempt to always include old names so that the plant is easily identifiable. And finally, a plant's cultivar, which are often referred to as 'variety,' will always be noted in single quotation marks. For example, *Narcissus* 'Ariel.' There are not many references to cultivars in the book, and the few that appear are included only because I want you to know something unique about that particular cultivar.

✽ You will see that some plants will have several floriographic meanings, and sometimes they are contradictory to each other. This is common, because this dictionary, as well as its full online version, includes comprehensive references that include meanings from all over the world, and through many years. So, when selecting and deciphering plant material to create your gardens and gifts, always simply disregard meanings that don't feel appropriate to your overall message or desired sentiment. Instead, choose the meanings that carry your message in the truest sense.

For an ongoing, updated, fully comprehensive dictionary, please visit modernfloriography.com. This is where the whole *New Language of Flowers Dictionary* is housed. It is continuously updated with additional information, new hybrid flower meanings, and will offer ongoing appropriate and cohesive information on the language of flowers and floriography.

A

Acacia, aka wattle, yellow acacia, thorn tree	chaste love, concealed love, friendship, beauty in retirement, elegance, endurance of the soul, immortality, platonic love, purity, resurrection, secret love, sensitiveness
Agapanthus, aka lily of the Nile	love letters, love, enduring spiritual beauty and purity
Agave	tree of life (Mexico), abundance, security
Ageratum, aka floss flower, whiteweed	undying affection, politeness, delay
Alder	protection, symbol of appearance and glamour
Alfalfa, aka lucerne	life, breath of life
Alyssum, sweet	worth beyond beauty, excellence beyond beauty, exemplary modesty
Amaranthus+, aka amaranth	immortality, fidelity, everlasting friendship, never-fading flower, unwithering, endless love
American elm, *Ulmus*	dignity, grace, patriotism
American linden	marital virtues, conjugal love, matrimony
Arbor vitae, *Thuja occidentalis*	unchanging friendship, live for me, tree of life
Ash, *Fraxinus americana,* and *Fraxinus excelsior*	grandeur, expansion, greatness, growth, health, higher perspective
Asphodel, Narthecium ossifragum	my regrets follow you to the grave, memorial sorrow, languor
Astilbe	I'll still be waiting, worldly pleasures

THE NEW LANGUAGE OF FLOWERS DICTIONARY

Auricula+	painting, pride of newly acquired fortune, wealth is not always happiness
Avocado, tree and fruit	love, relationship, romance, sexual romance

B

Bamboo	loyalty, steadfastness, strength, good fortune, luck, protection, rendezvous, steadfastness, strength, wishes
Barberry, *Berberis*, **aka pepperidge bush**	sourness of temper, sharpness, ill temper, petulance, satire
Basil, sweet, *Ocimum basilicum*	kingly, royal, highly spiritual, good luck, best wishes, hatred
*Bassia**, **aka silver kochia**	adaptable, rugged for survival, resilient, orderly
Beautybush*, *Kolkwitzia amabilis*	outstanding beauty, abundance, highly productive, efficient, kind exuberance
Beech tree, *Fagus*	prosperity, lover's tryst, personal finances
Bells of Ireland	whimsy, good luck, gratitude
Bellwort, *Uvularia grandiflora**, **aka merry bells, cornflower, throat root**	promise, anticipation, a smile, hope, eagerness, I'm in suspense
*Bergenia**, **aka pigsqueak, elephant-eared saxifrage, elephant's ears, large rockfoil**	humor, joy, amusement, meticulous, prim, courteous, unchanged demeanor
*Berzelia lanuginosa**, **aka common button bush**	humility, modesty, sincerity, admiration, I am shy
Bird of Paradise, aka crane flower	joyful, magnificence, a symbol of faithfulness

Birch, *Betula*	graceful, meekness, self-sacrifice, devotion, rebirth, protection, purification, new beginnings, adaptability, dreams, elegance, growth, initiation, renewal, stability, transformation, pioneer spirit
Bleeding heart, *Dicentra*	undying love, unrequited love, elegance, fidelity, fly with me
Bluebell, English and Spanish, *Hyacinthoides non-scripta*, **aka common bluebell**	constancy, humility, kindness, gratitude, sometimes grief, delicacy, grateful, gratitude, luck, solitude, sorrowful regret, truth
Bonsai, topiary	stability, strength
Borage, *Borago officinalis*	abruptness, bluntness, bravery, rudeness
Boronia	sweetness, lively personality, softens the heart
Bottle Brush*, *Callistemon, Melaleuca*	abundance, laughter, joy, birth, new and sustaining life
Bougainvillea, **aka paper flower, Santa Rita, triplet flower**	a beauty, beautiful day, paper, paper flowers, correspondence
Box, *Buxus*	constancy in friendship, stoicism, ancientness, constancy, indifference
Breath of heaven, *Coleonema, Diosma*, **aka confetti bush**	your simple elegance charms me, good for nothing, usefulness
Bromeliad, *Bromeliaceae*	beauty, charm, elegance, success in life, success in love, wealth
Bush monkey flower*, *Mimulus aurantiacus, Diplacus aurantiacus,* **aka sticky monkey flower**	conquer adversities, clear-sighted, firm stance, unwavering kindness, insight, sustained beauty, optimism through adversity

THE NEW LANGUAGE OF FLOWERS DICTIONARY

Butterfly pea, *Clitoria ternatea*, **aka Asian pigeonwings, bluebell vine, blue pea**	feminine power

C

Cabbage	profit, self-willed
Cactus	warmth, maternal love, endurance, my heart burns with love, grandeur, enduring love, ardent love, bravery, burns with love, chastity, lust, protection, sex, my heart dreams come to fruition, you left me
Caladium	delight, great joy
California Poppy, *Eschscholzia californica*	sweetness
Canna	glorious, magnificent beauty
Cannabis sativa+, *Cannabaceae*, **aka hemp, marijuana, grass, gallow grass, kif**	fate, blessings of fate, hardiness, roughness
Cape Jewels*, *Nemesia*	vibrant personality, fun, whimsical, opulent affection
Caryopteris, **aka bluebeard**	delightful presence
Ceanothus*, aka wild lilac	reliability, rarity, constancy, vibrant personality
Cedar	strength, prosperity, longevity, long life, drives away negative energies, goals, I live but for thee, think of me
Cercis, **aka redbud tree**	love tree, sometimes betrayal

*Cerinthe**, aka honeywort, pride of Gibraltar, blue shrimp plant	tenacity, constancy, enduring, timeless affection
Cestrum, aka night blooming jasmine	transient beauty, gift from God
Cherry blossom	a good education, sweetness of character derived from good works, insincerity, ascetic beauty, feminine beauty, gentle, honor of graceful resignation, kind, peace, spiritual beauty, transience of life, transience of melancholy
Cineraria	ever bright, always delighted, you are my delight, singleness of heart
Citronella	protection, cleansing, man's love, healing
Clarkia, *Godetia*, aka satin flower	your witty conversation delights me, pleasing, enthusiasm, charming, farewell to spring, fascination, sincerity, love flower, will you dance with me?
Clary sage, *Salvia sclarea*	clarifying, clear the mind, cool, lift the spirit, uplifting
*Clethra**, aka sweet pepperbush, summer sweet	generous, favorable, brave, talented
Convolvulus major, *Ipomaea purpurea*, aka morning glory	extinguished hopes, affection, bonds of love, departure, greet the new day, busybody, coquetry, embrace, glorious beauty, humility, I attach myself, love in vain, coquetry, death, death and rebirth, she loves you, spontaneity, willful promises
Coral bells, *Heuchera*	challenge, hard work
Coreopsis	always cheerful, love at first sight, impatience of happiness, impatient of absence
Corn*, *Zea mays*, aka maize	spiritual blessing, fertility, abundance, sustenance, ancestral honor, health, symbol of life, renewal, good luck

THE NEW LANGUAGE OF FLOWERS DICTIONARY

Crabapple blossom	overcomes irritability
Crepe myrtle, *Lagerstroemia*	eloquence
Cypress, *Taxodium distichum*, **all species**	death, mourning

D

Daisy+, *Bellis,* **all species**	innocence, simplicity, beauty
Daphne odora, **aka winter daphne**	painting the lily, make beautiful that which is beautiful, unnecessarily adorn, desire to please, fame, glory, I would not have you otherwise
Darling Pea*, *Swainsona*	bold yet graceful, a lady in every way, resilient, graceful beauty
Datura stramonium, Datura metel, **syn. moon flower, thornapple, jimsonweed, devil's trumpet**	delusive beauty, disguise, deceitful charms, suspicion **Highly toxic, poisonous to humans and animals**
Daylily, *Hemerocallis*	wealth and pride, success, flirty, coquetry, diversity, tenacity
Deutzia*	delicate and ample beauty, exuberant grace, lavish, charm, elegance
Dicentra+, **aka bleeding heart**	undying love, unrequited love, elegance, fidelity, fly with me
Digitalis, **aka foxglove, fairy caps, fairy thimbles, Our-Lady's-glove, witch's thimble**	stately, youth, insincerity, a wish, deception, I am ambitious only for you, mystery, occupation, youth
Dill	soothing

***Diosma*, aka breath of heaven, confetti bush**	your simple elegance charms me
Dittany of Crete, *Origanum dictamnus*, aka hop marjoram	birth, love
Dogwood, American, *Cornus florida*	faithfulness, duration, durability, charm, finesse, indifference, I am indifferent to you

E

***Eryngium*, aka sea holly**	attraction, independence, severity
***Eschscholzia californica*, aka California poppy**	sweetness
***Eucomis**, aka pineapple lily**	epiphany, prideful, majestic, deceptive charm
***Euonymus*, aka spindle tree**	long life, your charms are engraved on my heart, likeness, your image is engraved on my heart
***Eupatorium*, aka Joe Pye weed**	delay, love, respect, horror
***Euphorbia*, aka spurge**	purification, protection, persistence, welcome, hope in misery
Everlasting daisy *Xeranthemum*, aka annual everlasting, eternal flower, paper daisy	unfading remembrance, cheerful in adversity, eternity, immortality
Everlasting pea, *Lathyrus latifolius*	lasting pleasure, an appointed meeting, go not away, wilt you go with me?

F

Fern+, primary	fascination, sincerity, magic, shelter

THE NEW LANGUAGE OF FLOWERS DICTIONARY

Fir tree+, *Abies*	time, height, cleverness, adaptability, ability to change, spirit of the forest
Flower of Oahu, *Sida fallax*	hello, royalty, welcome
Foxglove, *Digitalis*	stately, youth, insincerity, a wish, deception, I am ambitious only for you, mystery, occupation, stateliness, self-ambition
Fritillaria imperialis, **aka imperial lily, crown imperial**	majesty, power, pride of birth, arrogance
Fuchsia	humble love, good taste, confiding love, amiability, faithfulness, frailty, frugality, love secrets, my ambitious love plagues itself, taste, the ambition of my love thus plagues itself
G	
Gardenia jasminoides, **aka cape jasmine**	ecstasy, feminine charm, transport of joy, I'm too happy, you're lovely, secret love, refinement, emotional support, exhilarating emotions, good luck, healing, love, peace, purification, purity, spirituality, sweet love, transient joy, transport of joy, transport to ecstasy, you are lovely
Garland of roses	reward of virtue
Garlic	protection, strength, get well, courage, ward off evil and illness
Germander speedwell, *Veronica chamaedrys* **aka bird's-eye speedwell**	facility, the more I see you, the more I love you, fidelity
Geranium farreri, **hardy or wild, aka cranesbill, storksbill, Farrer's crane's-bill**	constancy, availability, I desire to please, envy, wishes come true, imbecility, steadfast piety, deceit, fertility, folly, friendship, frustrations passing away, gentility, health, joy, preference, protection, returning joy, stupidity, true friend

Goat's rue	reason
***Godetia**, **Clarkia**,* **aka satin flower**	your witty conversation delights me, pleasing, enthusiasm, charming, farewell to spring, fascination, sincerity, love flower, will you dance with me?
Grape+, vine and fruit	domestication, hospitality

H

Hawthorn tree, *Crataegus,* **aka English hawthorn, may flower, may tree, thorn apple**	hope, love and marriage, banishes strife, protection, chastity, contradictions, duality, hope, male energy, spring, union of opposites
Hebe, *Hebe speciosa*	beloved, favored, keep this for me, I dare not, keep this for my sake, always fun!
Hemerocallis, **aka daylily**	wealth, success, pride, coquetry, diversity, tenacity
Hemp; flowers*	euphoria, therapeutic, medicinal, power to heal, precaution, mindfulness
Hibiscus, flower, including 'flower of an hour' annual *Hibiscus trionum*	delicate beauty, tropical love, consumed by love
Holly, berries	Christmas joy, protection
Hollyhock+	healing, forgiveness, ambition, fecundity, devotion to love, fertility
Hoya, **aka wax plant**	sculptured loveliness, constancy, pure loveliness
Huckleberry	faith, simple pleasures, simple leisure

Hyacinth+, primary	games, play, sport, constancy, flower of Apollo, gay flower, pure loveliness, joyful love, jealousy, benevolence, constancy, faith, gentleness of nature, happiness, impulsiveness, love, overcoming grief, protection, rashness
Hydrangea, **shrub (given as plant)**	devotion to a noble cause or love, unveiling

I

Ice plant, *Ficoides*, **aka dew plant, fig marigold**	old beau, rejected, your looks freeze me, idleness, coldhearted, rejected addresses
Ivy+	constancy, fidelity, friendship, wedded love, affection, matrimony, reciprocal, dependence, endurance, fidelity, friendship and fidelity in marriage, happy love,

J

Jack-in-the-Pulpit, *Arisaema*	continued happiness, love springs eternal
Jacob's ladder, aka blue-flowered Greek valerian	grace and elegance, wealth, come down, rupture, split
Jasmine	amiability, transport of joy, I am so happy, wealth, grace, friendliness
Jasmine, Carolina	separation, far country
Joe Pye weed, *Eupatorium*	delay, love, respect, horror

Juniper, *Juniperus,* **aka gin plant, gin berry**	protection, welcome to new home, aid, asylum, love, succor

K

Kalanchoe	popularity, endurance, lasting affection, eternal love, persistence, your temper is too hasty
Kennedia, **aka coral vine, scarlet runner**	mental beauty, intellectual beauty
Kerria japonica,* **aka Easter rose, Japanese kerria, yellow rose of Texas**	pleasant through the years, mature grace, perpetual beauty, be tough but stay beautiful, long beautiful
Kumquat, branches with fruit	symbol of good fortune, wealth, health, and happiness

L

Lagerstroemia, **aka crepe myrtle**	eloquence
Lamb's-ears, *Stachys byzantina,* **aka woolly betony, donkey's ears**	softness, support, surprise
Lantana	rigor, severity
Lemons and limes	fidelity in love, zest, divine healing, removes sadness, brings affection
Lent lily, aka wild, naturalized daffodil	sweet disposition
Leucojum, **aka snowbell, snowflake, dewdrops, St. Agnes' flower**	herald of spring, purity, hope

Lichen	dejection, solitude, confidence
Lilac, wild*, *Ceanothus*	reliability, rarity, constancy, vibrant personality
Lily+, general	fruitfulness, purity, majesty, wealth, Chinese emblem for Mother, honor, purity of heart, innocence, devotion, beauty, birth, exalted and unapproachable, humility, magnificence, modesty, religious pride, supreme, sweetness and humility, utility of heart
Lily, *Eucomis**, **aka pineapple lily**	epiphany, prideful, majestic, deceptive harm
Lily of the Nile, *Agapanthus*	love letter, love, enduring spiritual beauty and purity
Lily-of-the-valley, *Convallaria majalis*	delicacy, purity, return of happiness, humility, love's good fortune, you've made my life complete, perfect purity of the heart, happy tears of the Virgin Mary, Christ's second coming, fortune in love, trustworthy, unconscious sweetness
Lime, tree and flowers	conjugal love, wedded love, matrimony, fornication
Lisianthus	showy, kind thoughts, outgoing
London pride, *Saxifraga x urbium*	frivolity, fun, gaiety, lightheartedness, fortitude, refusal to submit, resistance
***Loquat*, aka Japanese medlar plum**	pure and ardent love, personal warmth and comfort
Love-in-a-mist, *Nigella*	you puzzle me, perplexity, bewilderment, independence, prosperity, delicacy, embarrassment, kiss me
Lucerne, aka alfalfa	life, breath of life

Lungwort, *Pulmonaria*, aka Bethlehem sage, spotted dog	thou art my life, you are my life
Lupine, *Lupinus*	voraciousness, imagination, dejection

M

***Magnolia+*, all species**	beauty, perseverance, sweetness, dignity, love of nature, benevolence, noble spirit, nobility, magnificent and splendid beauty
Mallow flowers*+, *Malva arborea, Malva*, aka tree malva, annual mallow, bush mallow	protection, love, and fertility, resilience, safety, security
Maple	elegance, reserve, love, retirement, draws together
Maple tree, entire tree	success, abundance
Maple, Japanese	baby's hands
Marguerite daisy	variety, oracle of the meadows
Marigold	health, sacred golden light, flower of Mary, Mary's gold, overcomes grief, despair, jealousy, pretty love
Marigold, French	comforts the heart, overcomes jealousy
Marijuana, *Cannabis sativa, Cannabaceae*, aka hemp, grass, gallow grass, kif	fate, blessings of fate, hardiness, roughness
Mignonette, *Reseda*	your qualities surpass your charms, health, worth, happiness of the moment

Mimosa, aka sensitive plant, mimosa tree, Persian silk tree	sensibility, delicate feelings, prudery, secret, chastity, bashful modesty, secret love, fastidious, exquisite, sensitivity
Mistletoe	I surmount all difficulties, I want to be kissed, kiss me, affection
Morning glory, *Ipomaea purpurea, Convolvus major*	extinguished hopes, affection, bonds of love, departure, greet the new day, busybody, coquetry, embrace, glorious beauty, humility, I attach myself, love in vain, death, and rebirth, she loves you, spontaneity, willful promises
Moss+	maternal love, charity
Mushroom+, any kind	suspicion, surprise
Myrtle, *Myrtus*	fidelity, love, marriage, married bliss, passion, Hebrew emblem of marriage, love in absence, remembrance, love positive, good deed, heartfelt love, immortality, joy, memory of the Garden of Eden, mirth, modest worth, money, peace, sacred love, scent of the Garden of Eden, souvenir of the Garden of Eden, symbol of the Garden of Eden

N

Nandina, aka heavenly bamboo	my love will grow warmer
Nasturtium+, aka Indian cress	patriotism, jest, a warlike trophy, resignation, victory
*Nemesia**, aka cape jewels	vibrant personality, fun whimsical, opulent affection
Nettle, *Urtica dioica*	slander, you are spiteful, you are cruel, don't sting me
Nigella, aka love-in-a-mist	you puzzle me, perplexity, bewilderment, independence, prosperity, delicacy, embarrassment, kiss me

O

MODERN FLORIOGRAPHY

Oats	music, I love your music, you satisfy me, soul of music
Olive tree	peace, fruitfulness, security and money, wisdom
Orange blossom	bridal festivities, your purity equals your loveliness, brings wisdom, chastity, eternal love, purity, generosity, married, magnificence
Orange, fruit	symbolic of golden pieces, good luck, fortune
Orlaya*, *Orlaya grandiflora*, **aka white lace flower, Minoan lace**	life's most delicate matters, many blessings, universal love, rejuvenation, guardian
Oxalis, **aka shamrock**	Ireland, joy, lightheartedness, luck, wit, loyalty

P

Palm	victory, dignity, success, fertility, peace, spiritual, the tropics, vacations
Peach	feminine softness, longevity, bridal hope, generosity, gentleness, happiness, peace, riches young brides, your qualities, like your charms, are unequaled
Peach, flowering	I am your captive, love, divination, longevity, long life, my heart is yours, I am yours
Pear, fruit	affection, health, hope, longevity
Pear, blossom	affections, lasting friendship, more than just lovely
Pear tree	comfort
Peperomia, **aka radiator plant, baby rubber plant**	everything will be as it should be, what is to be will be
Persimmon	resistance, bury me amongst nature's beauty

THE NEW LANGUAGE OF FLOWERS DICTIONARY

Phlox	proposal of love, sweet dreams, unanimity, our souls are united, united hearts, united souls
Pineapple Lily*, *Eucomis*	epiphany, prideful, majestic, deceptive charm
Pineapple sage, *Salvia elegans*	hospitality, happy home
Pistachio, tree and nuts	good fortune, happiness, health
Plantain	pilgrimage, well-trodden path
Platycodon, **aka balloon flower**	return of a friend is desired, honesty, obedience, unchanging love
Pleniflora*, *Kerria japonica* **aka Easter rose, Japanese kerria, yellow rose of Texas,**	pleasant through the years, mature grace, perpetual beauty, be tough but stay beautiful, long beautiful
Plum, fruit	promise, hope, hope for tomorrow
Plum tree	fidelity, longevity, beauty, genius, keep your promises
Poinsettia	be of good cheer
Pomegranate	good luck, elegance, sometimes foolishness, royalty
Poppy+, *Papaver orientale*	eternal sleep, oblivion, imagination, pleasure, consolation, wealth, dreaminess, fantastic extravagance, death
Princess flower, *Tibouchina semidecandra*, **aka glory bush**	patience, beauty, timeless beauty, glorious beauty, glory
Pulmonaria, **aka lungwort, Bethlehem sage, spotted dog**	thou art my life, you are my life

Pussy willow, *Salix*	never-ceasing remembrance, motherhood, recovery from illness, receiving a blessing, spring, in Asian cultures: symbol of luck, prosperity, good fortune, love

Q

Quaking grass	agitation, my thoughts are uneasy
Queen of the prairie, *Filipendula rubra*	farsighted outlook

R

***Ranunculus*, garden, aka Persian buttercup**	attraction, charming, you are rich in attractions, I am dazzled by your charms, pride, ambition, childhood reminiscence, childishness, fascination, ingratitude, memories of childhood, perfidy, riches, social matters, you are radiant with charms
Raspberry	gentle-heartedness, remorse, scornful beauty, temptation
Redwood*, *Sequoia sempervirens*	robust, durability, ingenious, resourceful
Rhubarb	advice
***Rudbeckia,* aka black-eyed-susan**	justice, impartiality, love conquers all, pure-minded

S

Safflower	marriage, welcome
Sage+	domestic virtue, skill, wisdom, greatest wisdom and respect, long life, gratitude, eliminates negative energy, esteem, wisdom, alleviates grief, good health, immortality, agelessness
Sage, purple-leaf	gratitude

THE NEW LANGUAGE OF FLOWERS DICTIONARY

Sage, pineapple, *Salvia elegans*	hospitality, happy home
Salvia sclarea, **aka clary sage**	clarifying, clear the mind, cool, lift the spirit, uplifting
Scotch thistle	retaliation, alerting, Christ's deliverance, hard work, suffering
Sequoia, *Sequoiadendron giganteum*, **aka giant sequoia, giant redwood, Sierra redwood**	long life, vast wisdom, perspective, health, protection, growth, durability, longevity, valor, enlightenment, eternity
Service berry	harmony
Shamrock, *Oxalis*	Ireland, joy, lightheartedness, luck, wit, loyalty
Sida fallax, **aka flower of Oahu**	hello, royalty, welcome
Silene, *Silene dioica*	youthful love, I fall victim
Smilax	loveliness and constancy, mythology
Snapdragon	strength, gracious lady, power of will, presumption, no, never!
Snowberry	heavenly thoughts
Snowflake, *Leucojum*, **aka snowbell, dewdrops, St. Agnes' flower**	herald of spring, purity, hope
Sorrel, wood	maternal love, secret sweetness, parental affection, joy, maternal tenderness
Speedwell, germander, *Veronica chamaedrys*, **aka birds-eye speedwell**	facility, the more I see you, the more I love you, fidelity

Spider Plant, *Anthericum*	antidote
Spiderwort, *Trandescantia virginiana,* **aka Virginia spiderwort**	felicity, happiness, transient friendships
Spirea	conceit, victory
Spurge, *Euphorbia*	purification, protection, persistence, welcome
Statice, Limonium, **aka sea-lavender, statice, caspia, marsh-rosemary**	never-ceasing remembrance, sympathy, lasting beauty
Sticky monkey flower*, *Mimulus aurantiacus, Diplacus aurantiacus,* **aka bush monkey flower**	conquer adversities, clear-sighted, firm stance, unwavering kindness, insight, sustained beauty, optimism through adversity
Strawberry	goodness, perfect goodness, esteem, love, luck
Sunflower	adoration, loyalty, you are splendid, best wishes, adoration, false riches
Swainsona*, **aka darling pea**	bold yet graceful, a lady in every way, resilient, graceful beauty
Sycamore	growth and persistence, curiosity, hopes and cares, curiosity, grief

T

Tendrils, any climbing plant	ties that bind
Trillium	modest ambition, modest beauty
Truffle, ground fungi	surprise

Tuberose, *Agave amica*	dangerous love, voluptuousness, dangerous pleasures
Tulip+	charity, fame, happy years, memory, declaration of love, famous, renown, perfect lover, flower emblem of Holland
Tulip tree, *Liriodendron*, aka canoewood, tulip poplar	fame, rural happiness

U

Uvularia grandiflora*, aka large-flowered bellwort, merry bells, cornflower, throat root	promise, anticipation, a smile, hope, eagerness, I'm in suspense

V

Valerian, aka all-heal, common valerian, English valerian, garden valerian, cat's valerian	an accommodating disposition, facility, good disposition
Veronica, aka speedwell	female fidelity, fidelity

W

Walnut	intellect, strength of mind, healing, protection
Wax plant, *Hoya*	sculptured loveliness, constancy, pure loveliness
Weigela	accept a faithful heart, grace and yielding to love
Wheat	friendliness, prosperity, riches, wealth, you will be rich
White lace flower*, *Orlaya grandiflora*, syn. Minoan lace, orlaya	Life's most delicate matters, many blessings, universal love, rejuvenation, guardian

Wild lilac*, *Ceanothus*	reliability, rarity, constancy, vibrant personality
Willow, weeping	mourning, sadness, bravery, sometimes forsaken love, melancholy, bitter sorrow, forsaken
Winged seeds, all sorts	messengers, spirit message from nature
Wisteria, *Wisteria frutescens,* **aka American wisteria and** *Wisteria floribunda,* **aka Japanese wisteria**	Daughter's sweetness, welcome stranger, cordial welcome, I cling to thee, love, poetry, protection
Wood sorrel, *Oxalis corniculata*	joy, maternal tenderness

X

***Xanthium*, aka cocklebur**	pertinacity, rudeness
***Xeranthemum*, aka annual everlasting,** *everlasting* **daisy, eternal flower, paper daisy**	unfading remembrance, cheerful in adversity, eternity, immortality

Y

Yarrow, *Achillea millefolium,* **aka woundwort**	cure for heartache, heals wounds, health, sorrow (in times of war) to dispel melancholy and heartache, war, courage, love, psychic powers, courage, healing, heartache
***Yucca*, aka Adam's needle**	there is life, abundant and hardy life, natural charms

Z

***Zea mays**, aka maize, corn**	spiritual blessing, fertility, abundance, sustenance, ancestral honor, health, symbol of life, renewal, good luck

PART 5
Quick-Start *Directories*

The quick-start directories are designed to be a fast and helpful go-to reference when you are thinking of a particular occasion or feeling that you would like to connect with or send off to another person. As a reminder, you do not need to attach all the meanings of the flower or plant—you can if you would like to—but you can also select only the meaning or meanings that are most appropriate to your overall message. This is just a guideline and meant to spark your inspiration and tap into your own thoughts and feelings. Get creative!

Quick-Start Occasions Directory

Use this list to see some of the flowers and plants that are most representative of a particular occasion.

ENGAGEMENT

- **American linden;** conjugal love, matrimony, marital virtues
- **California poppy,** *Eschscholzia californica;* sweetness
- **Eriostemon*,** *Philotheca myoporoides;* my beloved, dear to me, loved
- *Kalanchoe;* popularity, endurance, lasting affection, I protect you, tolerant heart, a happy notice
- **Plum,** blossom; be of good cheer, keep your promises, fidelity
- **Sweet William,** *Dianthus barbatus;* love, affection, classic love flower, boldness, pure affection, childhood, memory, grant me one smile, perfection, finesse

NEW JOB OR CAREER

- **Geranium,** penciled or skeleton; ingenuity, good health
- **Indian hawthorn*;** versatility, honesty, industrious, energetic
- **Mulberry,** black, tree or fruit; wisdom, prudence
- **Pink, China,** white-color, *Dianthus chinensis,* aka Indian pink; ingenious, talent
- **Pussy willow,** Asian traditions; symbol of luck, prosperity, good fortune, love
- **Wax myrtle,** *Myrica,* aka bayberry, bay-rum tree, candleberry, sweet gale; good luck, instruction, discipline, duty

GRADUATION

- **Baby blue eyes,** *Nemophila menziesii*; success, prosperity, safety, security, open heartedness
- **Bay laurel, wreath;** reward of merit
- **Bells of Ireland;** whimsy, good luck, gratitude
- **Dusty miller;** felicity, delicacy, venerable, industriousness
- **Elder**; zealousness, compassion
- **Fennel;** force, strength, worthy of praise

NEW HOME OR LIVING ENVIRONMENT

- **Cordyline,** aka good luck plant, palm lily, Hawaiian ti plant; majesty, honor, purity of heart
- **Grape;** domestication, hospitality, charity, intemperance
- **Holly;** domestic happiness, goodwill, protection, symbol of life, rebirth, enchantment, foresight, defense
- **Jade plant/tree,** *Crassula ovata*; symbol of good fortune, wealth, health, happiness
- **Jerusalem sage,** *Philomis*; earthly delights, pride of ownership
- **Olive;** peace and prosperity

CHILDBIRTH

- **Dittany of Crete,** aka hop marjoram; birth, childbirth
- **Honeysuckle**; generous and devoted affection, chains of love, I love you, sweetness of disposition, bond of love
- **Hosta;** devotion
- **Nasturtium,** *Tropaeolum majus*, aka garden nasturtium, Indian cress, monk's cress, pastel shades; maternal love, charity
- **Rockfoils,** *Saxifraga,* aka mossy saxifrage; affection
- **Roses, 25 stems;** congratulations
- **White sage;** protection, health

ACHIEVEMENTS

- **Crocus, autumn;** aka saffron crocus; thankful, cheer as our finest days are passing, mirth, ancient symbol of the sun, cheerfulness, beware of excess
- **Daylily,** *Hemerocallis;* wealth and pride, success, flirty
- **Edelweiss,** *Leontopodium*; noble courage, daring, devotion
- **Hemp, flowers*;** euphoria, therapeutic, medicinal, power to heal, precaution, mindfulness
- **Iris,** aka fleur-de-lis; ardor, faith, eloquence, wisdom, promise in love, hope, valor, valued friendship, message, emblem of France, I burn with passion
- **Oak leaves;** bravery, strength, humanity

END OF LIFE

- **Everlasting,** *Helichrysum italicum,* aka immortelle; never-ceasing memory, perpetual remembrance, endless love
- **Geranium,** pink color; gentility
- ***Ginko biloba*,*** aka maidenhair tree; enlightenment, solitary beauty, profound endurance, longevity
- **Golden Alyssum,** *Aurinia,* aka basket of gold; tranquility
- **Grass;** submission, the fleeting quality of life, utility, usefulness
- **Huckleberry;** faith, simple pleasures

ILLNESS AND INJURY

- *Echinacea,* aka purple cone flower; capability, skill, strength, health
- *Eucalyptus*, aka gum tree; protection, purification, healing
- **Fig;** longevity, peace, prosperity, strength, energy, prolific
- **Ginger;** pleasant, safe, warming, comfort
- **Horehound;** virtue, fire, health, healing++
- **Mugwort,** *Artemisia vulgaris*; dignity, tranquility, awareness of our spiritual path

QUICK-START OCCASIONS DIRECTORY

Quick-Start
Sentiments Directory

Use this list to see some of the flowers and plants that are most representative of a particular feeling or emotion.

FEAR

- **Elderberry**, *Sambucus;* compassion, kindness
- **Garland of roses**; reward of virtue
- **Garlic chives**; courage, protection, strength
- **Geranium**, red color, scarlet geranium, aka wide malva; comforting, consolation, gaiety, gentility++
- **Harebell,** common, *Campanula rotundifolia,* aka lady's thimble; submission, grief, humility++
- **Hellebore**, aka Lenten rose, Christmas rose; relieves anxiety, protection against calumny, scandal, a beautiful year ahead

PRIDE

- **American elm**, *Ulmus;* dignity, grace, protection, patriotism, vigor
- **Dragon root**, *Arum dracontium* (green); ardor
- *Gloxinia*; a proud spirit, love at first sight
- *Hardenbergia**, aka coral pea, happy wanderer, vine lilac*;* spirited, happiness, capability, ingenuity
- **Pineapple**; you are perfect, perfection, luck
- **Rose,** centifolia, hundred-leaved; graces, pride

JOY

- *Caladium*; affection, cares, constancy, delight, disquietude, great joy, grief, health, jealousy, joy, misery, remembrance, the sun
- *Callistemon,* aka bottle brush; abundance, laughter, joy, birth, new and sustaining life
- **Heliotrope, Indian**, aka Indian turnsole; intoxicated with joy, intoxication of love
- **Hyacinth**, peach, apricot, pink, red colors; play, playful joy
- **Salad burnet**; a merry heart, happy mood
- **Wild grape;** charity, mirth, joy, gaiety

TROUBLED

- **Calcynia***, *Thryptomene, Baeckea imbricata* and *grandiflora, Kardomia,* aka grampians heath myrtle, calynia, heath myrtle; sustenance, diversity, opulence, abundance
- **Hibiscus**, shrub; peace, happiness, rare beauty
- **Hollyhock** (including *Malva*); healing, forgiveness, ambition, fecundity, devotion to love, mother of family
- **Honeywort***, *Cerinthe,* aka blue shrimp plant, pride of Gibraltar*;* tenacity, constancy, enduring, timeless affection
- **Hyssop;** *Hyssopus officinalis*; cleansing, purification, holy herb that wards off evil and evil spirits, holiness
- **Knotweed**, *Persicaria microcephala, Persicaria orientalis,* aka kiss-me-over-the-garden-gate; vigilance, restoration

HEARTBREAK

- **Eglantine**, *Rosa rubiginosa,* aka sweet briar; a wound to heal, a poetic person, poetry, simplicity++
- **French marigold;** comforts the heart, overcomes jealousy
- **Pleurisy root;** heartache cure
- *Plumeria*; shelter, protection

- **Rain lily,** *Zephyranthes,* aka autumn zephyr lily, fairy lily, magic lily, zephyr flower; healing, fond caresses, serenity++
- **Raspberry;** gentle-heartedness, remorse

EXCITEMENT

- **Allegheny vine,** *Adlumia* (native Minnesota wildflower, endangered), aka climbing fumitory; good nature
- **Carolina silverbell*,** *Helesia Carolina,* aka silverbell tree; surprise, epiphany, contentment, good fortune, prosperity, wonderment
- *Coleus**; intensity, excitement, energy, showy
- *Copaea*, aka cathedral bells vine, cup-and-saucer vine; exciting news, gossip, knots, or bonds of love
- **Salvia,** red color; excitement
- **Wild Sage*,** *Hemizygia,* aka candy kisses; cheerful, tenderness, sparkling personality, light-hearted, lively

ADMIRATION

- *Deutzia**; delicate and ample beauty, exuberant grace, lavish charm, elegance
- *Diosma*, *Coleonema pulchellum*, aka breath of heaven, confetti bush; your simple elegance charms me
- **Dogwood,** flowering; I admire your personality and social abilities, our love will endure adversity
- **Frankincense;** a faithful heart
- **Heather,** purple/lavender color; beauty, worthy of admiration
- **Silver-leaf geranium,** *Pelargonium sidoides*; recall, admiration, gentility

CONFUSION

- **Dock;** patience
- **Leucadendron**; steadfastness, loyalty, intent
- **Liverwort;** *Anemone nobilis, Hepatica;* confidence, trust, apathy, your love makes me happy, constancy, permanence
- **Rosemary;** devotion, fidelity, remembrance, wisdom, commitment, intellect, healing balm, constancy, stimulates healthy thinking and promotes well-being, your presence refreshes, good faith
- **Rue;** clear vision, grace, purification, repentance, can also mean disdain, fertility, manners
- **Serviceberry,** *Amelanchier*; harmony, agreement, prudence

Resource Directory

PLANTS AND SEEDS

There are a multitude of online-based companies that offer plants and seeds for sale. Above all, I encourage you to shop from your local nurseries and other outlets for seeds and plants, while keeping in mind to support the seed and plant companies that practice sustainability and offer non-GMO and heirloom varieties of seeds and plants.

Here are just a few of my favorite online companies, which I have patronized for many years and will continue to do so, mainly because of their commitment to sustainability but also for their quality and selection.

SIMPLY *Sustainable*

When sourcing and propagating seeds, please always choose to buy heirloom, and non-GMO seeds, preferably from a company that is committed to the Safe Seed Pledge, *"For the benefit of all farmers, gardeners, and consumers who want an alternative, we pledge that we do not knowingly buy, sell, or trade genetically-engineered seeds or plants."* The mechanical transfer of genetic material outside of natural reproductive methods and between genera, families, or kingdoms poses great biological risks and economic, political, and cultural threats. These genetically engineered varieties have not been sufficiently tested prior to public release. There are a host of other reasons to avoid genetically modified seeds and food-items as well, but the main concern is that until we know the long-term ramifications of toying with nature, it's not a good idea to cultivate, support, or especially consume these items. I don't believe any of us want to lose our heirloom varieties, but if we keep crossing them out repeatedly, we could potentially lose their pure, unaltered genetics forever. That's why it's so important to support companies that are focused on heirloom and non-GMO plants and seeds.

PLANTS

Annie's Annuals

Website: anniesannuals.com

An amazing and favorite place to buy annuals, unique and exotic plants, as well as bareroot trees and berries. The plant descriptions are always so informative and include native habitat and origins information, growing conditions, and more. Every spring, receiving Annie's mail order catalog with its colorful and engaging artwork is always a joy to me!

Digging Dog Nursery

Website: diggingdog.com

A retail and mail-order plant nursery specializing in unusual and hard-to-find perennials, ornamental grasses, shrubs, trees, and vines.

Geraniaceae

Website: geraniaceae.com

Pelargoniums and geraniums are very popular in floriography. Their sentiments are just perfect for most occasions, and they frame posies perfectly and can envelope a bouquet of roses like no other greenery. In the garden, they are absolutely perfect in every way, providing structure, texture, and a pop of color where needed. This website is highly educational and offers an unbeatable collection of pelargoniums and geraniums. Have fun shopping here!

Menagerie

Website: menagerieflower.com

Growers and purveyors of field grown garden roses, specialty flowers, French prunes, and more. Shopping on this site is feast for the eyes and senses as you'll find not only high quality bare root roses for nationwide shipping, but also gardening gear, gifts for the home, and floral design tools. They even have pre-cooled tulip bulbs and fresh flower bouquets, not to mention an incredibly informative and educational blog.

Heirloom Roses

Website: heirloomroses.com

A great mix of old gardens, heirlooms, and new introductions, combined with great educational articles and videos. Their roses are sold as bareroot, planted in gallon pots, so they can be a bit pricier, but the roses are shipped very nicely and can self-sustain for a few days in their planting mix while awaiting their final placement planting.

Izel Native Plants

Website: izelplants.com

A vast selection of native plants available for shipping throughout the Midwest and East Coast of the U.S., as far south as Georgia. On this website, there is a handy and informative tool that allows you to view the native plants that are available according to your own state (only those included in the shipping areas) or where the plant is native to.

Logee's Plants for Home and Garden

Website: logees.com

A favorite of mine for houseplants, primarily, but I have also bought many beautiful perennials and annuals from them. They do have a helpful printed catalog, as well, if you prefer.

Lyndon Lyon Greenhouses

Website: lyndonlyon.com

Lyndon Lyon has been growing, breeding, and selling African violets for more than seventy years, and it shows in their helpful customer service, quality, and selection.

Native Wildflowers Nursery

Website: nativewildflowers.net

Without native flowers, the insects, birds, and other animals that co-evolved with them cannot survive. This website is an incredible resource for wildflowers, perennials, ferns, and wetland plants. A handy feature is their zip code–based database, which will advise you whether or not the plant is appropriate for your zone and climate. And if the plant you want is not available to purchase from them, they direct you to nurseries that do stock the plant that you want.

Plant Lust

Website: plantlust.com

This is the most handy and informative site I have found to scout out nurseries for sourcing plants for your garden. You can shop for plants with the ability to select by plant types and styles, seasonal interest, soil types, habitat-specific plants, and much more.

Resendiz Brothers

Website: resendizbrothers.com

When I need more cut protea than I can grow, this is where I buy them from. The site is very informative and resourceful, anything and all about *proteas* including all genera. You can purchase both plants and cut flowers from this site.

The Growers Exchange

Website: thegrowers-exchange.com

Herb plants galore! So many herbs are used in the language of flowers, and this site is abundant with rarities that will ship right to your door.

The Tree Store

Website: thetreestore.info

A vast selection of trees, shrubs, bushes, vines, and ornamentals, and a really decent planting guide.

The Vermont Wildflower Farm

Website: vermontwildflowerfarm.com

This is a useful and valuable resource site to learn about and purchase all types of seeds, bulbs, plants, gardening, wildflower identification, and a thoughtful pet-friendly section as well.

SEEDS

Dawn Creek Farm

Website: dawncreekfarm.squarespace.com
A small family farm that breeds and grows specialty cut flowers—and also my friends and neighbors! The gorgeous Zinnias that you see on page 17 were grown and gifted to me by the incredible Dawn Creek Farm, and I cannot rave enough about the creativity and pure talent of Kori and her family. If you want some incredible, diverse, newly hybridized seeds, flowers, vegetables, and even natural dyes, this is your place.

Eden Brothers

Website: edenbrothers.com
A good selection of rare hybrid, organic, and heirloom seeds. They are supporters of the "Seed Integrity Pledge" and only work with growers who share the same stance against genetically modified seeds.

Johnny's Seeds

Website: johnnyseeds.com
Since 1973, this company has been providing high-quality seeds, with a broad selection of just about anything you could ever want to grow. They are one of the nine original signers of the Safe Seed Pledge, and this website is incredibly resourceful and includes an extensive grower's library.

Plant World Seeds

Website: plant-world-seeds.com
Specializing in rare, unusual, and exotic seeds for flowers, trees and shrubs, grasses, and vegetables. The website lists valuable information and education on natives, invasive species, and toxicity.

Rare Seeds

Website: rareseeds.com
Also known as Baker Creek, founder Jere Gettle started Baker Creek Heirloom Seed Co. in 1998 as a hobby and has since grown into North America's largest heirloom seed company. They share a significant portion of their profits for emergency aid, sustainable development, providing food, and educating people in the U.S. and abroad. This site is not only a valuable resource for heirloom seeds but also offers copious information on growing, history of the seeds, and supplies, gifts, and tools.

Safe Seed Pledge

Website: safeseedpledge.org
This is a resource site that offers access to a large number of seed-safe companies that offer heirloom, non-GMO, organic seeds.

Southern Seeds

Website: southernseedexchange.com
I have been able to find obscure seeds from here, such as lemon bergamot (delicious addition to tea!) and peony duchess asters. There are copious amounts of seed collections, which is such a fun idea, as well as herbs, vegetables, flowers, plants, and fruits. They also have microgreens and sprouts too.

Territorial Seed Company
Website: territorialseed.com
Get the catalog! The catalog is so informative and unique, with copious varieties of non-GMO and organic seeds available for mail order or buy online from their website.

Victory Seeds
Website: victoryseeds.com
An extensive online catalog of non-GMO, rare, open-pollinated, heirloom seeds. More vegetables than flowers and herbs, but still a wonderful selection of great herbs and perennials.

Plant Care and Gardening Tools

Greenhouse Megastore
Website: greenhousemegastore.com
A vast offering of all garden supplies, including seed-starting, clippers, irrigation, greenhouse kits and supplies.

Grow Organic
Website: groworganic.com
Growing supplies, including tools and equipment, frost and sun protection, pest control—and even trees, plants, and seeds.

Planet Natural
Website: planetnatural.com
Filler, mulch, natural pest control, composting worms, and ladybugs! They also sell fertilizers, hydroponics, grow lights and more.

Gardening How-To and Plant Knowledge

American Horticultural Society
Website: ahsgardening.org
Articles and resources on landscapes and gardens. They have a sustainable gardening section, and a beautiful and informative newsletter that you can sign up for to receive garden tips and know-how from experts, event notifications such as garden tours, and more.

Epic Gardening
Website: epicgardening.com
A great site built with lots of well-written and user-friendly articles on gardening. And some articles have shop link buttons so you can easily purchase the seeds or plants they write about, in addition to links for raised beds, seeds, and soil care.

Garden Lady

Website: gardenlady.com

Website of C. L. Fornari, author of several gardening books, a consulting garden adviser, a wonderful newsletter, podcast, and radio show.

National Gardening Association

Website: garden.org

This is the official website for the National Gardening Association, which provides boundless information. Their mission is to promote gardening, and this website is incredibly informative and resourceful for all levels and interests in gardening and horticulture. The plant database is impressive, and I enjoy seeing the photos of new plants regularly uploaded by members.

The Spruce

Website: thespruce.com

You will see this website listed in the bibliography because it is such a great resource for so many things. Plants A to Z, landscaping, pests and problems, and a host of other how-to resources on this site. Bookmark this one!

Plants of the World Online

Website: powo.science.kew.org

As an international collaborative program freely available to all, this reference site is home to a digitized database of the world's flora, gathered from the past 250 years of botanical exploration and research. This incredible resource will guide you to a plant's taxonomy and includes plant descriptions as well as images. I view this site as an authority on plant names, species, subspecies, genus, origins, and everything in between and beyond.

Cut Flowers

Although the information that follows is primarily centered and focused on the United States and Great Britain, the locally grown philosophy and its principles applies to anywhere in the world.

The idea is to prompt and encourage sustainability, and to be environmentally, socially, and economically minded with our buying and consumption in general. And, in order to support environmental, economic, and social change for the better, it is vital that we support our local, regional flower farmers. Here is how your flower-buying process should take place, and in an order of sourcing:

1. Buy from flower farms local to your town or within a hundred miles. Farmers markets are wonderful sources, and an increasing number of flower vendors are selling at these markets. Local, independently owned flower shops should have access to locally grown flowers, too, so always ask! Local flower growers that co-op and create hubs for sourcing their blooms to local flower shops and floral designers are on the rise and implanting in major cities and regions nationwide, so check for those co-ops in your closest, more urban locations. More than likely they will offer a public buying day or daily hours.

2. If not directly local to you, make sure your flowers come from farms located within your region or state.
3. And finally, if you cannot buy flowers grown in your own state, then purchase flowers grown in the country you live in.

National Farmers Market Directory

Website: nfmd.org
Use the locater tool found on the NFMD website to locate a farmers market near you. These should be your first and foremost source for the freshest and most beautiful locally grown flowers. Most local flower growers will have a stall that they will occupy and sometimes share with other growers. Remember, the more direct support we can give to our flower farmers, the more sources and varieties we'll have!

Slow Flowers™

Website: slowflowers.com
Slow Flowers is the long-respected wellspring of local flower sourcing. This website is a large and comprehensive directory of flower growers, florists, studio designers, event designers, workshops, classes, gatherings, summits, and more, all local to you and at your fingertips. This is also a wonderful place to read about what a *slow flower* is, and why it's important.

Alaska Peony Collective

Website: alaskapeonycooperative.com
Need some peonies? During July and August, this amazing collective of Alaskan peony growers can ship them to you nationwide.

Public Wholesale Flower Markets

If you live in a place that has a flower market nearby, lucky you! Just be sure to ask where the flowers are grown, and also, and I know it's hard, but please try and only buy flowers that are in season. They will be a true statement that you want to adhere to the seasonality and locality aspects of flowers, *flowers at their best.*

UK-Based Directories

Flowers from the Farm

Website: flowersfromthefarm.co.uk
The UK's primary and comprehensive directory of flower farms, studios, as well as florists who sell British-grown flowers.

From Britain with Love

Website: frombritainwithlove.com
A beautiful blog and resource site that includes select flower growers and makers of all kinds, a creative workshop directory.

British Flora

Website: britishflora.co.uk

A incredibly informative site and supplier of native wildflower plants and seeds with intention and focus on actively improving habitats across the diverse landscapes of the United Kingdom.

Materials and Methods Sources

I am constantly discovering new things and evolving my repertoire of high-quality and unique materials and resources for creating gorgeous botanical-oriented gifts. Please visit my website at **teresasabankaya.com** for associate shopping links, and be sure to follow me on social media, and sign up for my newsletter, where I offer the latest references and resources for where you can purchase all the materials that I've used in this book, as well as day-to-day creations and developments. See the About the Author page for web links and social media handles.

Additionally, here are some of my tried-and-true resources for material and tools that I have and continue to use for creating posies and other gifts.

eBay

Website: ebay.com

I use it as a source for natural wood picks for crafting, as well as vintage and new trumpet vases, mint juleps, goblets, etc.

Chrysal Arrive Alive Eco Bouquet Wraps

Website: chrysalflowerfood.com

This is an eco friendly source for bouquet hydrating wraps that I use for posies and bouquets that are going to be transported without a water source for some time. Arrive Alive® Eco is an eco-friendly flower wrap which creates a water reservoir for cut flowers. The flower wrap and bag are made from renewable resources and are fully compostable.

Etsy

Website: etsy.com

A wide array of unusual items such as vintage ribbons, one-of-a-kind vases, handmade papers, and so much more. It is wonderful to support independent artisans and small businesses through this site, and they have made it easy and streamlined to do so. I have purchased so many different unique and beautiful things from Etsy, and many are seen here in this book!

Gardener's Supply Company

Website: gardeners.com

This website is a large and comprehensive shopping source for all sorts of gardening supplies and tools, including clippers, snips, watering cans, and gloves. They are a company run by gardeners, so they've thought of virtually anything and everything. Many times, I've purchased things that I didn't know I even needed!

Michaels

Website: michaels.com

If you've ever seen one of my posy presentations, then you've heard me talk about Michaels. Either shopping in the store or online, they are North America's largest provider of arts, crafts, floral, scrapbooking, textile arts, and merchandise for makers and do-it-yourself arts and crafters. Simply put, most of the crafting materials you find in this book can be sourced at Michaels, at one level or another.

Niwaki

Website: niwaki.com

Niwaki is a Japanese lifestyle brand dedicated to gardeners and craftspeople. They have an incredible assortment of very high quality and well-designed floral scissors and snips.

OLMS Bamboo Floral

Website: olmsbamboofloral.com

OLMS Bamboo Floral's mission is to provide eco-friendlier, highly functional, and beautifully designed floral supplies to the eco-minded floral customer. Currently, they offer bamboo sticks that can be used to attach sentiment tags to posies when you don't want to use a ribbon. I am happy to support this company, as they are focused on eco-friendly floral supplies that are used regularly by professional florists, as well as novice designers.

VASES AND CONTAINERS

Etsy

Website: etsy.com

Again, Etsy wins with their incredible selection of vintage or new stemware and particularly lovely options for something very unique and one-of-a-kind.

kRi kRi Studio

Website: etsy.com/shop/krikriceramics

The sweet vase you see the chocolate cosmos in on page 7 is a bud vase made by Kristin Nelson's Seattle-based studio.

Wayfair

Website: wayfair.com

A global online source for all things *home* with a substantial collection of stemware available. If you just search *glass water goblets* you will find many various styles and colors.

Madonna Inn

Website: shopmadonnainn.com/goblets

Home to the famous signature Madonna Inn glass water goblets. They are absolutely my favorite! You can see I have used some of them in photos in *The Posy Book* (pages 53, 64, and 104).

Sentiment Tag Crafting Paper and Wrapping

Please visit my website, **teresasabankaya.com** for complementary or paid sets of downloadable sentiment tags, ribbon and embellishment kits for sale, and more.

The sentiment tags available on my website are available in Word or PDF format, and once you've downloaded them, all you'll need to do is to fill them in and then print from home.

The ribbon and embellishment kits are put together in beautiful themes and coordinating textures and colors and include all you need to make several different sentiment tags with harmonizing ribbons.

Both the sentiment tags and the kits are a handy and affordable way to keep posy tags and crafting materials available to you without having to buy large quantities of one thing.

Additionally, here are sources that I have used for many years to procure materials for sentiment tags and wrapping.

Etsy

Website: etsy.com

In the search bar, just type *embellishments* and have fun!

Floral Supplies

Website: floralsupplies.com

In addition to tools, this site always has a nice selection of wrapping supplies, such as tulle and mesh fabrics, and waterproof paper for wrapping bouquets.

Mulberry Paper and More

Website: mulberrypaperandmore.com

Any kind of paper you can imagine, including natural wrapping papers and mulberry paper sized for printing.

Paper Source

Website: papersource.com

A longtime favorite of mine with a vast and varied selection of all sorts of paper, notecards, die-cut shapes, stickers, specialty papers, and even workshops.

Scrapbook.com

Website: scrapbook.com

Papers, die-cuts, stickers, and you can even shop by theme. This site teeming with all things sentiment tag making. If you don't have any idea how to jazz up your gifts, just browse this site for inspiration.

The Spent Rose

Website: etsy.com/shop/thespentrose
This is a wonderful Etsy shop offering a mix of textiles, handwoven appliqués, vintage trims, antique lace, ribbons, and baubles that are absolutely perfect for exquisite sentiment tag embellishing.

Vintage Passementerie

Website: vintagepassementerie.com
From the same proprietor of The Spent Rose, this shop is perfect for when you want to add elegant, true vintage flair to your designs. Some of the offerings are vintage French brocade ribbon, French ombré antique ribbons, appliqués, all sorts of needlework and laces, and so many more unique, gorgeous collections.

Wrappily

Website: wrappily.com
Recycled and recyclable, double-sided eco wrapping paper along with very pretty cotton curling ribbons.

OTHER HELPFUL RESOURCES

American Horticultural Therapy Association

Website: ahta.memberclicks.net
The American Horticultural Therapy Association (AHTA) is the only national U.S. organization advocating for the development of the horticultural therapy profession and the practice of horticulture as therapy for human well-being. AHTA supports the professional development, education, and expertise of horticultural therapy practitioners. Their website is very informative and gives access to a database where you can find a certified horticultural therapist in your area. Also, with an optional membership to the association, it provides information on members-only events, an online magazine, education, and many more resources.

Audubon

Website: audubon.org/native-plants
The above website link directs you to Audubon's bird-friendly native plants guide. All you do is enter your email address and zip code, and the database will provide you a list of native plants to your area that are bird-friendly, and even what types of birds the plant will attract, as well as a where to buy link.

PLANT CLUBS AND SOCIETIES

Our plant-specific societies and clubs are invaluable resources to us, and these websites include copious articles and resources on the care of the plants and resources how to propagate, sell, buy, social events, competitions and shows. They provide the ability meet others that have the same interest in the specific genre of plants that you do and will often hold swaps and other opportunities to collaborate and meet new friends.

African Violet Society of America

Website: africanvioletsocietyofamerica.org

A nonprofit educational organization for African violet enthusiasts. Learn about plants, join the society, shop for supplies, and participate in events and contests. This is an excellent and extensive source of learning how to grow African violets, troubleshooting, and propagating. They even have an Ask an Expert feature on their website with a quick answer to any question you may have.

American Daffodil Society

Website: daffodilusa.org

The American Daffodil Society (ADS) is a nonprofit educational, organization supported by memberships and donations. The ADS is open to everyone from hobbyists and beginning gardeners to experienced botanists and daffodil experts. Their website is brimming with all you would ever need to know about daffodils with resources for shopping, clubs, events, and lots of fun facts too. They also host a family of other daffodil websites, including an online library at dafftube.org.

American Dahlia Society

Website: dahlia.org

An extremely informative site covering the fundamentals of growing *Dahlias* for use as cut flowers. Learn about diseases, care, and maintenance, and virtually anything else dahlia. The resources for *Dahlia* clubs throughout the nation are wonderful because these clubs almost always have annual tuber sales where you can acquire your tubers most suited to your climate.

American Rose Society

Website: rose.org

Established in 1892, The American Rose Society's mission is to promote the culture, preservation, and appreciation of the rose and to improve its standard of excellence through education and research. The website is chock-full of information, including a list of nationwide, regional rose societies and their events, and of course, a phenomenal resource directory for everything from identifying roses, caring, purchasing, and anything in between.

Bibliography

BOOK SOURCES

Beales, Peter. *Classic Roses*. Henry Holt and Company, 1997.

Connolly, Shane. *The Language of Flowers*. Rizzoli International Publications, 2004.

Mancoff, Debra N. *The pre-Raphaelite Language of Flowers*. Prestel Verlag, 2003.

Quealy, Gerit. *Botanical Shakespeare: An Illustrated Compendium of All the Flowers, Fruits, Herbs, Trees, Seeds, and Grasses Cited by the World's Greatest Playwright*. Harper Design, 2017.

S. Theresa Dietz. *The Complete Language of Flowers: A Definitive and Illustrated History*. Wellfleet Press, 2020

Sabankaya, Teresa. *The Posy Book: Garden-Inspired Bouquets That Tell a Story*. The Countryman Press, 2019.

Stuart-Smith, Sue. *The Well Gardened Mind: Rediscovering Nature in the Modern World*. William Collins, 2020.

Internet Sources

ancientegypte.blogspot.com
annieandre.com
archive.org
bachflowerlearning.com
balconygardenweb.com
bardgarden.blogspot.com
bbc.com
berkeleywellbeing.com
floranorthamerica.org
bhg.com
bible.org
bonsaitreegardener.net
botanicalinstitute.org
britanica.com
classicalwisdom.com
collinsdictionary.com
digitalcollections.nypl.org
drawpaintacademy.com
epicgardening.com
evolutionaryherbalism.com
extension.umn.edu
farmersalmanac.com
florgeous.com
gardenia.net

gardeningknowhow.com
gardens.si.edu
harvesttotable.com
healthline.com
healthyfocus.org
history.com
joincake.com
landscapeplants.oregonstate.edu
leafyplace.com
longfield-gardens.com
medicalnewstoday.com
merriam-webster.com
minnesotawildflowers.info
motherearthliving.com
museodelprado.es
ncbi.nlm.nih.gov
outdoormoss.com
petalrepublic.com
plantcaretoday.com
plants.ces.ncsu.edu
positivepsychology.com
powo.science.kew.org
shunspirit.com
simplicable.com

study.com
succulentalley.com
suestuartsmith.com
theecologist.org
thegraphicsfairy.com
theimpatientgardener.com
thepreraphaelitepleasaunce.substack.com
thespruce.com
treehugger.com
treesandshrubsonline.org
treesforlife.org.uk
utopia.org
vnps.org
wikipedia.com
worldhistory.org

About the
Author

Teresa Sabankaya is a florist, gardener, teacher, presenter, and author. Her floral studio has been providing professional floral design services for elegant lifestyles and events in the Monterey Bay and San Francisco Bay Area for over thirty years, designing florals for daily enjoyment, weddings, and other milestones. She is most notably recognized for the creation of her modern-day posies, which are garden-style bouquets that tell a story in the language of flowers.

Her work has been featured in numerous Hoffman Media publications, including *Victoria* magazine, *The Art of Flowers*, and *Living with Roses* as well as in *Country Gardens*, *Elle*, and *Sunset* magazines, and *The New York Times*. Additionally, her wedding and event flowers have been highlighted in industry media outlets such as *Green Wedding Shoes*, *Brides magazine*, *Grey Likes Weddings*, and many more. She has been an annual participant in the prestigious Bouquets to Art, DeYoung Museum at Golden Gate Park, and Monterey Museum of Art. She is also very active as a presenter and speaker at flower and garden shows, garden clubs, and various other flower and garden-themed events nationwide. Her annual Posy Atelier and Garden Parties are highly popular events that she hosts in her garden as well as at other locations.

Teresa lives in and runs her floral studio in Bonny Doon, a special little enclave set among the redwoods in the Santa Cruz Mountains, with her husband, Nezih, and their fur baby girl, a Frenchie named Violet. She has two grown daughters who live nearby. She enjoys any time spent in the garden and especially loves to entertain there with her friends and family.

Teresa would love it if you would stay in touch with her. Here's how:

Teresa's main website, **teresasabankaya.com**, is where you can shop for posies and much more, all delivered nationwide. You can also sign up for her newsletter, titled *Gifts from the Garden*, which she sends quarterly and is filled with floral beauty, inspiration and insight, as well as a schedule of upcoming events, and of course, loyalty discounts.

At **modernfloriography.com**, you'll find the comprehensive floral dictionary, which is updated regularly with new meanings for flowers that have been around for a while, and also newly introduced hybrids. When you don't have either of her books handy, just pop in and learn the meanings of over 2,000 flowers and plants!

Social media platforms: Facebook, Threads, LinkedIn & Instagram @teresasabankaya.

Newsletter on Substack: teresasabankaya.substack.com